The Rise and Fall of Explorys and IBM Watson Health

In 2015, Explorys was a healthcare intelligence cloud company that had built one of the largest clinical data sets in the world, representing more than 50 million lives. It provided secure cloud-based solutions for clinical integration, at-risk population management, cost-of-care measurement, and pay-for-performance. The acquisition of Explorys complemented and strengthened the IBM Watson Health Cloud platform and empowered IBM's vast ecosystem of clients, partners, and medical researchers to surface new connections among diverse and previously siloed healthcare data sets. The combination of both Explorys and IBM Watson Health was expected to spur the creation of a new generation of data-driven applications and solutions designed to advance health and wellness. So, what went wrong?

IBM Watson Health is a massive case study in healthcare innovation gone awry. IBM was one of the oldest and largest technology companies in the world and was riding a tailwind with IBM Watson's Artificial Intelligence success on Jeopardy in 2011. The Watson Health division was seeded with multiple healthcare acquisitions, one of them being Explorys. Explorys had a portfolio of hosted population analytic solutions and the largest clinical dataset in the United States at the time, at approximately 50 million de-duplicated patients. The newly created division was loaded with potential and seemed destined for success. Yet Watson Health went from being founded in April 2015 to imploding in May 2018 in a little over three years and took Explorys down with it.

IBM Watson Health's ascent and descent were covered by both healthcare and mainstream media. Watson Health was self-described as IBM's "Moonshot" in healthcare. This venture failed, and it cost IBM billions of dollars. These were expensive lessons on managing innovation in healthcare, but also on managing innovation in general. This book chronicles the story of Explorys and IBM Watson Health and what led to its downfall in just three short years. Written by one of Explorys' founding engineers, the book relates the rise and fall of both Explorys and IBM Watson and provides a message for future tech entrepreneurs and IT managers alike.

The Rise and Fall of Explorys and IBM Watson Health

A Personal Memoir of a Healthcare Moonshot that Misfired

Doug Meil

Routledge
Taylor & Francis Group
A PRODUCTIVITY PRESS BOOK

Designed cover image: T&F

First published 2026
by Routledge
605 Third Avenue, New York, NY 10158

and by Routledge
4 Park Square, Milton Park, Abingdon, Oxon, OX14 4RN

Routledge is an imprint of the Taylor & Francis Group, an informa business

ISBN: 9781032793603 (hbk)
ISBN: 9781032793597 (pbk)
ISBN: 9781003491590 (ebk)

DOI: DOI: 10.4324/9781003491590

Typeset in ITC Garamond
by Deanta Global Publishing Services, Chennai, India

This book is dedicated to the staff, partners, and healthcare systems that made Explorys possible.

Contents

Foreword

Data has always been valuable to businesses. Your home insurer wants to measure weather and climate risk and needs to understand regional building costs. Credit card issuers need to know cardholders and vendors and to recognize unusual transaction patterns for both. And health care companies use individual patient and population data, as well as complex scientific data on diagnostics and therapies, to deliver care.

In the 1990s and 2000s, Google created technology that it used to index and organize the World Wide Web on a scale no one had ever attempted before. That technology eventually led to the powerful AI systems we see today. Along the way, though, other data-hungry industries learned how to use the same techniques for themselves.

One of the earliest to do so in the health care sector was Explorys, a spin-out from the Cleveland Clinic. Doug Meil was a key technical leader on Explorys' founding team. He and his colleagues took advantage of open-source implementations of Google's systems to capture, organize, and analyze vastly more medical data than had ever been used in one place previously.

Doug and I met in 2009. I was the founding CEO at Cloudera, delivering that Google-inspired software to the market. Doug was, I thought, one of the most interesting users of our products. He and his team were smart and ambitious.

Making health care better was (and is!) a really important problem. They were doing that in really innovative ways.

We stayed close during the years of Explorys' rapid growth as an independent company. We stayed in touch through the IBM acquisition and in the years since. He's still smart, ambitious, and doing interesting work!

Explorys certainly wasn't the only company that put vast data to novel use. It is, though, a great example: great technical founders, serious start-up energy, challenges and growth, an acquisition by one of the biggest players in the market, and an eventual divestiture of the business. Along the way, the team innovated constantly. Most of the cool uses of data in health care that I see today were foreshadowed for me by Doug and his team.

But I will let him tell that story!

Mike Olson is a serial technology entrepreneur with a long career in the database industry. In addition to co-founding Cloudera, he served as CEO of Sleepycat Software, acquired by Oracle, and was the co-author of BerkeleyDB. He worked as a software developer, and in sales and marketing, prior to becoming CEO. He holds BA and MSc degrees in Computer Science from the University of California at Berkeley.

Preface

IBM's Jeopardy project in 2011 put Artificial Intelligence (AI) back on the map. AI research had been around for decades, combining periodic advances with multiple "AI winters" and other reversals, but winning at Jeopardy was something that really looked, for lack of a better word, *intelligent*. This project was preceded by a number of other influential and successful IBM Research efforts, such as Deep Blue for chess in the 1990s. As complex as chess may be, Jeopardy was something else. Nerds played chess, but *regular people* could watch and play along with Jeopardy. Winning at Jeopardy required competing against multiple humans. It had to factor in betting strategies, fast buzzing, and do it in English. Jeopardy had answers, questions, and lots of facts. Surely, any computer system that could win at Jeopardy could do *anything*. IBM executives looked around for a way to productize the Jeopardy project and the AI engine called Watson at its core. This is where IBM Watson Health came from.

It took a few years, but it happened. Healthcare was experiencing an exponential growth in data and sorely needed innovation, and the opportunity seemed ripe. IBM Watson Health was created in April 2015 as a stand-alone division in IBM to focus on the healthcare industry, to much fanfare. It was the first time IBM *ever* created an industry-specific division. *The New York Times* covered the launch with "IBM Creates Watson

Health to Analyze Health Data" (April 13, 2015). The first sentence of this article summed it up – "IBM is taking its Watson artificial-intelligence technology into health care in a big way with industry partners, a pair of acquisitions and an ambitious agenda." Forbes was similarly optimistic with "More Watson Goodness, IBM Announces Health Focused Vertical" (April 16, 2015).

The plan was to build productized solutions, layer on plenty of IBM technology (including Watson), and take healthcare by storm. Healthcare was called *IBM's Moonshot* by IBM leaders, in the spirit of the Apollo space program. It was a big swing. It seemed like a sure thing.

But in three years Watson Health was very publicly in flames. The headlines were brutal:

- "Layoffs at Watson Health Reveal IBM's Problem With AI" – *IEEE Spectrum* (June 25, 2018)
- "IBM Watson Supercomputer Recommended 'Unsafe and Incorrect' Cancer Treatments, Internal Documents Show" – STAT News (July 25, 2018)
- "IBM Watson, Health Thyself: How IBM Overpromised and Underdelivered on AI Health Care" – *IEEE Spectrum* (April 2, 2019)

It didn't make any sense. How could Watson Health fall apart so fast?

IBM would sell off the remains of the division a few years after that, in January 2022. Exact numbers aren't public, but IBM is estimated to have lost approximately $5 billion on Watson Health. To put this in IBM-perspective, 2015 global revenues were $81.7 billion with $13 billion in strategic imperatives, so whatever the actual loss was – while it wasn't *fatal* – it wasn't a rounding error, either. A billion here, a billion there, it can add up to a lot of money. This was far more than just about money, though. It represented a failure of a strategic initiative, and a loss of a degree of prestige and credibility in the very industry it was trying to transform. And this from a company with a storied history in the development of computing.

It just didn't make any sense.

But there were clues.

IBM in the 2010s

Critical context is that by the time of the Watson Health announcement in April 2015, IBM had experienced 12 straight quarters of revenue decline. Multiple *years* of shrinking.

A MarketWatch story from April 20, 2015 titled, unsurprisingly for the time, "IBM Reports Another Revenue Decline" had several relevant observations:

- IBM is the middle of a corporation reinvention similar that is starting to feel a lot like its early 90s transition to a software and services company. The company is shedding unprofitable hardware businesses, as it pursues higher-margin fare in the realms of big data, security, cloud computing, and software and services for mobile devices.
- Big Blue also has been pushing sales of its Watson software. IBM's Watson data-mining technology has delivered high-profile results, famously winning at Jeopardy in 2011, but the path to revenue has been slow.
- 'Investors and users both see them on the wrong side of the fence when it comes to disruption," Mr. Milunovich said.

To be fair, IBM still managed to be profitable. But experiencing multiple years of revenue loss in the tech sector represented nothing less than an identity crisis. IBM was looking for the Next Big Thing, and it wanted and needed it now. Identity crises in the tech sector were not unique, as Apple was famously down to 3 months of cash in 1997 before its miraculous rescue and rebirth. On the other hand, Hewlett Packard – another stalwart of the tech sector – was going through a painful restructuring during this period. Sun Microsystems was arguably the hottest tech company of the mid-to-late 1990s before being ignominiously scooped up by Oracle in 2010 and relegated to footnote status. Everybody looks invulnerable until they aren't, and IBM was very much *not* looking invulnerable. That pressure was not incidental for Watson Health.

A *Financial Times* article from November 4, 2021 titled "IBM Sheds 25% of Its Business in Battle against Decade of Decline" after its Kyndryl spinoff, described how the rest of the decade played out. IBM's revenue had fallen every year since 2011, except for one year when it grew less than 1%. The Kyndril spinoff, which contained IBM's managed infrastructure services business, left the company with about *half* the $107 billion annual sales IBM had in 2011. Wall Street valuations weren't any better. A decade prior IBM and Microsoft were both had market valuations at just over $200 billion. By 2021 IBM's value had slipped by half, and Microsoft's grew 10x to $2.5 trillion.

There is no other way to describe it. Those numbers are not great.

There is another telling quote from the 2021 *Financial Times* article:

> "There are markets we put a lot of money in that didn't work out," Arvind Krishna, IBM's chief executive officer, said of its contraction. Speaking in a recent interview with the Financial Times, he added that the company's problem "wasn't a lack of investment". "It's execution."

With respect to Watson Health, I could not agree more.

So What Happened?

This book is an extension of a post I wrote for the Association for Computing Machinery (ACM) in April 2021 called "What Happened To Watson Health?" I came to IBM Watson Health from one of the acquisitions, a healthcare analytics company called Explorys, and the combined Explorys/Watson Health experience represented nearly a decade of my life. I felt an obligation to try to get the story out, and as far as I know my ACM post was the first *first-person* account of IBM Watson Health. Writing that post was equal parts bravery and stupidity, but it mattered to me because I believed in the mission. I fought, along with many others, very hard to try to make Watson Health work. It didn't have to end like that.

Writing about business failure is a challenge because as the saying goes, success has many fathers, but failure is an orphan. Most businesses would rather sweep accidents and misfires under the rug and move on. But that would be a mistake. Airplane crashes are studied for a reason, and it isn't for entertainment. It's about understanding *what* people knew and *when* to better determine what errors are recoverable and what aren't. Such reviews make flying safer for all of us. As Atul Gawande's book *The Checklist Manifesto* describes, even healthcare has been slowly adopting such processes, albeit somewhat grudgingly. Doctors don't like to be questioned, and especially by non-doctors. But such reflection is necessary, even if it hurts. *Especially* when it hurts.

This book is told from the perspective of Explorys. It is a memoir. My memoir. There were certainly parts of Watson Health that I didn't either see or see that closely. Explorys brought its own idiosyncrasies, drama, and a few demons to the party as well as startups aren't typically formed by those that are entirely sane or with motives as pure as the driven snow. As with any story re-telling, this book will be inherently incomplete in some respects. It won't contain everything. It can't describe everything.

As the story of IBM Watson Health is ultimately and unfortunately a tragedy, there will be aspects that IBM won't necessarily savor. But the fact that IBM Watson Health failed is incontrovertible – just look the headlines. This book will try to expand on *why* and what could have been done differently to save it. I have also tried very hard to keep critiques as fair as possible, and to contrast what was known publicly to what was happening behind the scenes. No individual names are cited unless those names were already in the press. Not everything in this book may make rational sense because the failure of Watson Health, on the surface, doesn't make sense. Yet it happened.

Figure P.1 Explorys employees taking a ballet break in one of the rehearsal rooms in the Old Cleveland Playhouse (2013). Permission from Jen Hearn.

Figure P.2 **Relief outside one of the old theaters at the Old Cleveland Playhouse (2013). Permission from Jen Hearn.**

Acknowledgments

I would like to thank all the test readers of this book, who were primarily former Explorys employees, as well as those who contributed Explorys Memories to the Appendix, and all those who gave their permission for images. Thanks also to Jen Hearn for her pictures of Explorys at the Old Cleveland Playhouse.

Additional thanks to Scott Burr for explaining the literary-architectural differences between writing articles and books, as he had written many of both. That was invaluable. Thanks to publisher Taylor & Francis/Routledge for taking a chance on this book. And to my family for believing me when I kept saying, "I'm working on my book." I really was. Here it is!

I would also like to thank all the readers of my 2021 Association for Computing Machinery (ACM) post "What Happened To Watson Health?" as well as the ACM for publishing it. Without that post, people would never have asked me, "so when is the book coming out?" Even if they were kidding, and they usually weren't, that put the idea in my head. I would also like to thank the ACM for publishing my other posts on software and technology, because that provided a critical outlet to build writing confidence.

Thanks to Eliza Strickland for her Institute of Electrical and Electronics Engineers (IEEE) *Spectrum* articles in 2018 and 2019 about Watson Health. Those articles did a good job of not just reporting the *news* of Watson Health but also reflecting on the magnitude of the story and putting it in context.

Lastly, thanks again to the staff of Explorys, partners, and healthcare systems who made it possible.

Explorys is dead, but let it not be forgotten.

Don't stop believin'.

About the Author

Doug Meil is a software engineer with extensive experience in data integration, data management, and analytic solutions. He has delivered solutions in the financial, cable/telecommunications, and healthcare sectors for over 30 years, with over 20 years in commercial software development.

Doug was the founding engineer of Explorys in 2009, which was acquired by IBM in 2015 as a foundational part of the newly formed Watson Health division. Doug founded the Cleveland Big Data Meetup in 2010, which at over 4,000 members became one of the largest and most active tech meetups in the Midwest, and he continued to organize it for over 14 years. He was voted an Apache HBase Committer in 2011 during the early days of the open-source big data ecosystem and Hadoop. HBase was created as an open-source version of Google's Bigtable, a distributed key-value datastore. He also has a half-dozen software patents, for those who are impressed by that sort of thing. Doug was also appointed an IBM Distinguished Engineer in 2016.Doug has written dozens of posts for the Association for Computing Machinery (ACM) on a variety of topics including software engineering, data management and governance, analytics, and organizational leadership. He has also written for the Healthcare Information Management and Systems Society (HIMSS).

Doug has a Practice Oriented Master's in Engineering from Case Western Reserve University and a BSB in Decision Sciences from Miami University.

Doug's list of publications can be found at:

https://www.linkedin.com/pulse/publications-doug-meil/

The author (at left) at a Cleveland Big Data Mega Meetup at the Cleveland Museum of Natural History, September 2024

Introduction

I stared at the rubble.

It was 2023 and I was at the Old Cleveland Playhouse at East 85th and Carnegie, just west of the Cleveland Clinic Main Campus. I stood outside the perimeter fencing, checking in on the demolition. It was an awful sight given the memories, yet irresistible. I had to pay my respects.

Explorys was a healthcare analytics startup that, in its time, had the largest clinical dataset in the United States. It operated from the Old Cleveland Playhouse from 2012 to 2016, and everywhere I looked, I saw places I once stood. I could see an orange bar that was in the center hallway of the second floor. That bar held giant panes of glass that had originally been the gift shop for the Cleveland Museum of Contemporary Art, the previous tenant in the space. But the giant panes of glass looked stylish so they were retained and subdivided into a conference room and offices. People had a tendency to walk face-first into those giant panes of glass, just as birds would smack into a shiny high-rise. It took years before somebody finally taped up giant blue X's on the panes to put a halt to further facial injuries.

The complex was long on personality but was an unusual place to work, to say the least. The reason that Cleveland Clinic bought the complex in 2009 was because the Cleveland Playhouse theater company moved downtown to Playhouse

Square. And a big reason they moved was that the Old Cleveland Playhouse was a maintenance nightmare. There were garbage cans on the third floor catching rain leaks from the roof. The first floor had a former restaurant that I had used several times for an area tech meetup that I ran, and the bar kind of smelled like dead rats, probably because of dead rats. But as long as you stayed away from the bar, the restaurant space was decent enough for a meetup. Using the space didn't cost extra. I could make it work. It was the Explorys way.

Nearly everybody complained about the air quality. There were dozens of tests showing that things were within limits, but it was never quite clear what *within limits* meant in a 100-year-old facility, and Lord only knew what was in the walls and vents. There were multiple fire alarms where the Cleveland Fire Department had to respond. Not drills … *alarms*. The basement, which had historically been used for theater prop storage, was sufficiently creepy to be regularly used by regional SWAT teams for room-clearing drills. SWAT Wednesday was the day that you knew it was unlikely something would happen to your car, limiting the risk of someone sawing off your catalytic converter to Mondays, Tuesdays, Thursdays, and Fridays.

But it wasn't just the building that drew me to the demolition, it was the people that used to work in it. I got connected in what would turn into Explorys in the Summer of 2009 in a skunkworks effort. I had worked with Charlie Lougheed and Steve McHale before at Everstream, but it was primarily through Charlie as we had also worked together before that at KeyBank on software projects. Charlie and I had overlapping and complementary strengths. Charlie had a good mind for business and seeing opportunities. I was a technologist who could identify and prioritize the *needs* from the *nice-to-haves* and turn product ideas into product realities. Charlie didn't sleep much, and any given morning could see him coming in with a mockup of new functionality he had worked out the previous night. Or he could have rearranged his furniture.

Again. Or he could have gone out for a ten-mile run when normal people would have been sleeping. Normal people like me, for example. But we were both driven to deliver, and that is why I wanted to work with him again.

I also wanted to do something that had the chance of a more substantial societal impact than Everstream. Everstream did some fairly technically interesting work for its time, but its ultimate customer was the cable industry. Cable companies operate nationally but are effectively local monopolies and didn't earn their reputation of doing the absolute minimum and charging the maximum by accident.

Lastly, I wanted to see a software company in Cleveland that was built to last. Cleveland deserved that. Why should Silicon Valley have all the fun?

So much potential.

Gone.

I shook my head.

Driving by you would never know one of the most innovative software companies in healthcare once worked in this pile of bricks.

Figure I.1 Old Cleveland Playhouse being demolished (2023).

Chapter 1

The Creation of Explorys

The Creation Story

The creation story of Explorys was described amply in the press.

> "Size matters," insists Dr. Anil Jain, a primary care doctor and a biomedical engineer. He invented Explorys's search technology and left the Cleveland Clinic to put it to bigger use, teaming up with a pair of data-savvy local entrepreneurs.
>
> **Cleveland Plain Dealer (February 11, 2013)**

> Explorys has grown steadily since it spun out of the Cleveland Clinic in 2009. Its platform is based on search technology designed by Dr. Anil Jain, a primary care doctor and biomedical engineer who wrote software to scan electronic medical records without identifying patients.
>
> **Cleveland Plain Dealer (January 26, 2015)**

DOI: 10.4324/9781003491590-1

> After piloting a version of the software at the clinic, Jain and his colleagues worked with Cleveland Clinic Innovations, the system's technology development arm, to expand and commercialize the product, called Explorys. In 2009, it was spun off by the Cleveland Clinic as a separate company.
>
> **Modern Healthcare (August 2015)**

> Founded by McHale, Charlie Lougheed and Dr. Anil Jain in 2009, Explorys sprung from technology developed and incubated at the Clinic.
>
> **Cleveland Plain Dealer (August 2016)**

> "We've built our platform under the wing of the Cleveland Clinic, and the architecture and knowledge and intelligence has been tremendous," said McHale.
>
> **Cleveland Plain Dealer (August 2016)**

In 2015 the Harvard Business School Club of Northeastern Ohio awarded Explorys its entrepreneurship award called the Dively Award after Explorys was acquired by IBM. Publisher Braun Ink (in 2015, "The Braun Group") developed a graphic corporate history in cartoon form for the award dinner.

Making Explorys a success was actually pretty simple. Explorys received some amazing code from Cleveland Clinic in 2009, built a company on it, and that was that.

Data integration was easy as data was just thrown at the platform and it went in. Sometimes the data was thrown left-handed. Sometimes right-handed. Sometimes behind the back, fancy-style. Once in a while, it was tossed in with a fade-away while invoking a favorite basketball player's name. But integration was never a problem. Data always went in with a swish.

Figure 1.1 Explorys Graphic Corporate History by Braun Ink (2015).

The code that Explorys received just worked out of the box, and it had all the functionality Explorys needed, even though it had been designed years before. Performance tuning? Not needed. Scaling? Same. Security? Hackers didn't dare try because there were coffee cups with Explorys logos

Figure 1.2 Explorys Graphic Corporate History by Braun Ink (2015).

at the ready. Compliance? The software was so smart it self-complied.

In fact, the software never even had to be upgraded. Most of the people at Explorys just watched the lights on the servers blink when they weren't engaged in Nerf-gun fights or eating pizza.

There has never been an easier innovation story.

But there is another quote worth examining. The Cleveland Clinic published a book in 2014 called *The Cleveland Clinic Way*. It even had an endorsement from President Obama on the front cover, although his quote seems to refer to the Clinic itself rather than the contents of the book. There were even a few pages on Explorys:

> Stephen and Charlie licensed Dr. Jain's application and scaled it up, using a new architecture that could handle even more data from more sources. Eventually, Explorys grew into an enormous version of the search engine that Dr. Jain had developed for eResearch.

That passage, while attempting to add to the myth-making, raises some interesting questions.

What does "a new architecture" mean? Does it indicate a new design? An entirely different approach?

What does "handle even more data" mean? Were there limiting factors in the original application?

What does "from more sources" mean? Wasn't the original application functionally complete to everything Explorys needed?

So many questions from such an innocuous statement.

How could Explorys be simultaneously built on "a new architecture," but then also "based on search technology designed by Dr. Anil Jain" and "technology developed and incubated at the Clinic" as in the other quotes?

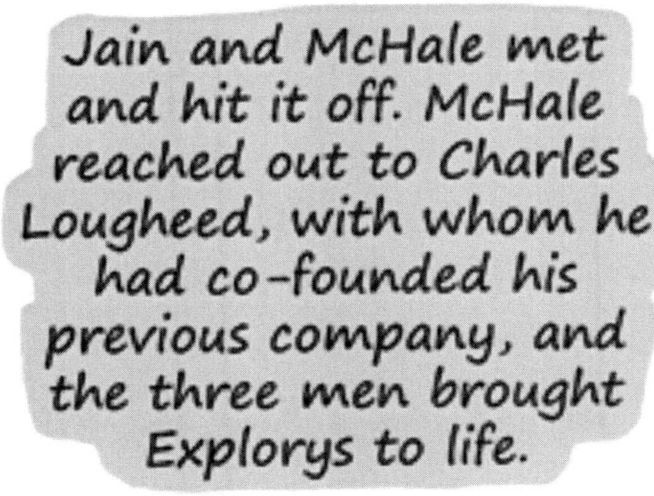

Figure 1.3 Explorys Graphic Corporate History by Braun Ink (2015).

It does make a person think.

Lastly, who could have been doing this work? The graphic corporate history had the same story as the other articles and press releases:

"and the three men brought Explorys to life."

Whether or not those three alone "brought Explorys to life" is questionable. But certainly, to do all the work involved described in *The Cleveland Clinic Way,* it sounds like there may have been at least four people at Explorys. I was certainly one of them. In Braun Ink's defense, they were only working with the information available to them at the time when they were commissioned for the graphic corporate history. The same goes for the people behind the Dively Entrepreneurship Award. That *was* the creation story of Explorys that was promoted.

Per the passage in *The Cleveland Clinic Way*, there may be more to the Explorys creation story than meets the eye. But this happens all the time, as creation stories become creations themselves.

The Creation of Creation Stories

People love a good creation story, and science and technology are full of them: somebody discovers or invents something and then the rest is history. It is seemingly *inevitable*. Real life, however, is rarely that clean. Modern calculus was created independently by Newton and Leibniz. The theory of evolution was conceived independently by Darwin and Wallace. Who gets the credit? Complexity tends to hurt our primate brains, and we gravitate to simpler stories to make sense of the world. One thing. One name. One banana for the reward. Inevitably, it won't be the whole story, but it's *a* story that can fit in our heads.

Creation stories that describe collaboration can be even more problematic. The structure of DNA is credited to Watson and Crick, but as Walter Isaacson's book *Code Breakers* described, while they didn't exactly steal Rosalind Franklin's X-ray diffraction images of DNA, they didn't exactly get her permission either. Although Franklin didn't come up with the double helix structure, her research provided critical evidence for it. Watson, Crick, and Wilkins were awarded a Nobel Prize in 1962 for this work, and Franklin conveniently died in 1958, thereby preventing a Nobel ethical dilemma due to the rule that there can be a maximum of *three* names per Nobel Prize. Four inventors were a crowd, and five were simply not allowed. Nobel Prize winners must also be among the living, so the DNA credit problem was solved as far as the Nobel Committee was concerned.

COBOL is a programming language created in the late 1950s that has long been utilized as the "business programming language" in numerous industries. The story that "Grace Hopper invented COBOL" emerged shortly thereafter to the everlasting annoyance of those who actually created the language. COBOL was created by a committee called CODASYL for the US Defense Department and was attempting to resolve the fact that there were *already* multiple "business" programming languages (even in the 1950s) such as COMTRAN (created by IBM) and FLOW-MATIC (which was created by Grace Hopper at Remington Rand), plus another proposed language AIMACO for the Air Materiel Command, for example. Jean Sammet, who was on the original committee and subsequent development, wrote multiple books on the history of programming languages and also served as president of the Association for Computing Machinery. She felt compelled to write an IEEE article called "The Real Creators of COBOL" in 2000, stating while she had immense respect for Hopper's work on the Harvard Mark I and FLOW-MATIC, Hopper was *not* on the committee that developed the language. And that wasn't even the first time Sammet tried to set the record straight. Yet the "Grace Hopper as COBOL inventor" story got out there and took root. While Hopper has many fans (including Sammet and myself), it didn't appear that she did much to clarify her involvement and that COBOL was far from a solo effort.

Creation stories often become creations themselves, sometimes accidentally, and sometimes deliberately. That was certainly the case at Explorys.

Chapter 2

The Actual Creation of Explorys

Timeline of Events

- Explorys/IBM Watson Health
  - *2009 – Explorys created in partnership with Cleveland Clinic Innovations*
  - *2009 – Explorys moves into its first office at 11490 Euclid Avenue*
  - *2010 – Explorys moves into Cleveland Clinic's new Global Cardiovascular Innovation Center (E. 100th and Cedar Road)*
  - *2012 – Explorys moves into Old Cleveland Playhouse (8501 Carnegie Avenue)*
  - *2014 – Explorys begins multiple acquisition conversations*
  - *2015 – IBM acquires Explorys, IBM Watson Health division created*
  - *2016 – Explorys moves into 1111 Superior Avenue*
  - *2018 – Mass layoffs in IBM Watson Health division*

DOI: 10.4324/9781003491590-2

  - *2018 – Explorys moves into a new building on E. 105th and Cedar Road*
  - *2022 – IBM sells remains of Watson Health*
  - *2022 – Last remaining Explorys services are de-commissioned*
- Other Events of Note
  - *2004 – Google MapReduce paper*
  - *2006 – Google Bigtable paper*
  - *2006 – Amazon AWS released*
  - *2006 – Hadoop framework created*
  - *2008 – Hadoop Summit, first conference*
  - *2009 – Hadoop World, first conference*
  - *2009 – Meaningful Use introduced as part of HITECH*
  - *2010 – Microsoft Azure Released*
  - *2015 – Cleveland Clinic Innovations Director fired for fraud*
  - *2015 – Cleveland Clinic/Theranos Partnership announced*
  - *2015 – First New York Times investigative article on Theranos*
  - *2017 – UnifyProject Cleveland*
  - *2018 – Blockland Cleveland*
  - *2020 – Covid-19 Pandemic*
  - *2023 – Old Cleveland Playhouse Demolished*

The Prototype

What Explorys licensed from Cleveland Clinic was the eResearch prototype and access to the data behind the prototype. The second part of the prior sentence "and access to the data behind the prototype" is kind of important, and we shall return to that point later.

The eResearch prototype was a web application for population searching. Development on it was performed by a single individual over about a year or two, and when I got involved in the skunkworks research in the Summer of 2009 before Explorys was formed, eResearch hadn't had any further development since the end of 2008 and was at a dead end.

It was based on a Microsoft technical stack with a single SQL Server database at the core, and the search table in the database contained a bitset of searchable attributes that could be evaluated to TRUE or FALSE. There were 909 concepts (e.g., "diabetes," "heart failure") defined that could in turn be bucketed into timeframes (e.g., "ever," "last 3 years," "last year"), so the resulting searchable bitset had the concept and timeframe cross product (e.g., "diabetes ever," "diabetes last 3 years," etc.), so in total, there were a few thousand "bits" that could be searched in the web application.

The rules were hard-coded based on the primary data source's data model, which was the Epic Data Warehouse product called Clarity – Epic being the vendor for the electronic medical record that Cleveland Clinic utilized. eResearch

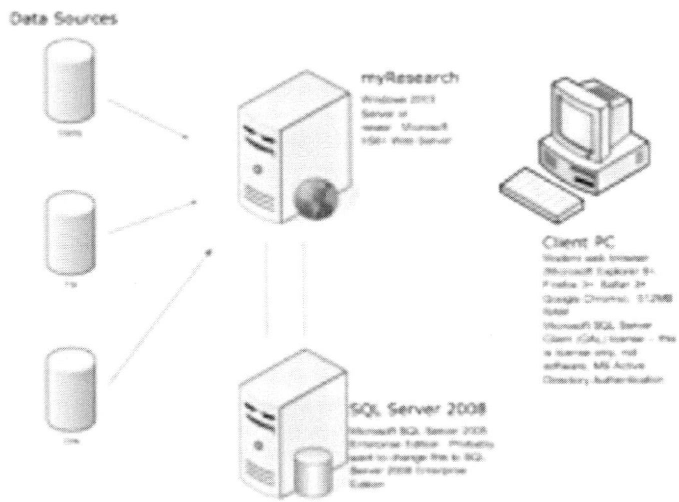

Figure 2.1 Cleveland Clinic – eResearch business proposal (2008) description of the technical architecture (non-distributed, single SQL Server database). Permission from Cleveland Clinic Innovations.

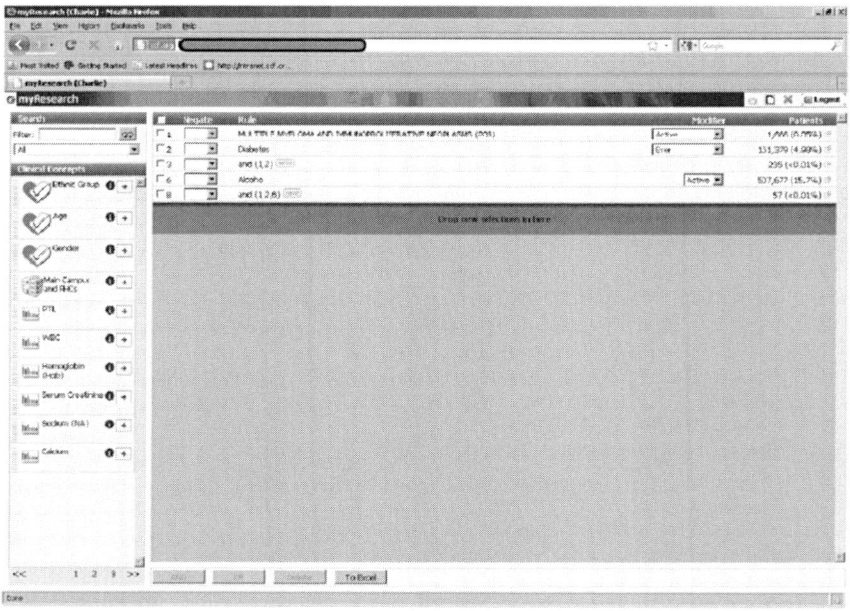

Figure 2.2 Cleveland Clinic – eResearch screenshot (2009 screenshot). Permission from Cleveland Clinic Innovations.

was being used somewhat in the Medicine Institute where Dr Jain worked, but not enterprise-wide at the Clinic. eResearch *was* a use case demonstrating the utility of population searching, however, which was something. But as development had ceased on eResearch, it wasn't going anywhere.

Cleveland Clinic Innovations typically licensed medical innovations, such as medical devices or related techniques. Licensing *software* or information technology was a very different animal, so to speak. When Explorys was negotiating the spinoff in 2009, there was only one other software spinoff from Cleveland Clinic that I was made aware of – some sort of business dashboard if memory serves – so this was new territory. More significantly, Explorys was the first Cleveland Clinic Innovations deal where *data rights* were included. That was *huge*. Data rights were the real innovation of the Explorys spinoff.

Word-Aligned Hybrid

"You should look at Word-Aligned Hybrid," said Todd Lipcon. It was October 2009, and Todd, who was a software engineer at Cloudera, threw this out with a casual brilliance that I would come to learn was his standard mode of operation. He would become legendary in the Hadoop ecosystem for diagnosing complex problems in one chat channel and somehow also diagnosing a completely different complex problem for another project on another channel. He was somehow fast, accurate, and comprehensive seemingly all at one and all the time.

What was Todd was referring to was Word-Aligned Hybrid Compression for Bitmap Indices. There were a number of reasons why Explorys couldn't base anything on the eResearch codebase (I documented this not just in 2009 at the formation of Explorys but also during the IBM acquisition process in 2015, see the Appendix), but most notably the bitset approach that eResearch used wouldn't scale for our purposes. Say, for example, there are 50 "bits" in a bitset like this:

0010000010000001000100100100000100000010001001000001100
Each bit – pardon the pun – takes a little bit of memory, and the above example is only one row.

The notion of bits to represent concepts that are on/off or true/false dates effectively to the invention of the bit itself. Papers from Claude Shannon and John Tukey in the late 1940s used the phrase, but there were centuries of older mechanical or electrical "bit" technologies, ranging from punch-cards for looms to stock tickers to Morse Code. The security command chmod, which appeared in 1971 in Unix, utilizes power-of-2 bits to represent file system permissions.

The 1-bit for executable, the 2-bit for write only, and the 4-bit for read only. Combinations of permissions could be assigned by setting multiple bits (e.g., 5 = executable and read only). Bitsets work well for squeezing a surprising amount of information into small places and scale pretty well, up to a point. Bitsets worked with eResearch, although it only supported a few thousand "bits" per patient and a relatively small number of patients. The Explorys vision was to support tens of millions of patients and to have the ability to search over a vast number of searchable concepts, perhaps a million or more per patient. Additionally, eResearch was built specifically for Cleveland Clinic and was not designed to handle the governance of multiple customers on the same platform, which is referred to as "multi-tenancy" support.

These were just some of the issues that made it clear eResearch, though an interesting prototype, wasn't going to be the base of Explorys' architecture.

Word-Aligned Compression worked by not just storing a bitset in compressed form, but also enabling bitset evaluations without having to decompress the data, which can be expensive in multiple ways especially if this function is repeatedly required. *Without having to decompress the data:* these are the kinds of details that software engineers get excited about. With typical compression schemes the data must be *de*compressed to be utilized, which takes extra CPU cycles and more memory. This doesn't mean that compression isn't useful – quite the contrary because it can save on storage as well as potential network transfer when data is stored remotely. But it's an extra cost. Compressed bitsets allow not just for a smaller memory footprint depending on the run-lengths (e.g., how many consecutive 0s and 1s), but also allow evaluation of the bitset while still compressed. At scale things like this matter. Word-Aligned Hybrid Compression was created at the Lawrence Berkeley National Laboratory a few years before that conversation for physics research because the lab needed better methods for locating extremely narrow signals in a large spectrum. Although Explorys didn't wind up using Word-Aligned Hybrid Compression, the suggestion got me thinking in a completely different direction about the potential of compressed bitsets.

The Hadoop Ecosystem

The reason I was talking to Cloudera is because I was at the first Hadoop World conference in the Roosevelt Hotel in New York in October 2009.

Explorys started at a fortuitous time: the Hadoop project had started in 2006 just a few years earlier. Hadoop was an open-source big data family of frameworks, itself inspired from a number of Google technical papers such as Google File System (distributed storage for large files), MapReduce (programming framework for distributed processing), and BigTable (distributed datastore for random reads, inserts, and updates). These were scale-out frameworks for workloads on *commodity hardware* – another key point. One didn't need to base a solution architecture on a single server, as even very large servers still have an upper limit. Ten servers provided 10x storage capacity and processing power as one server. Twenty servers provided twice as much capability as ten servers. And so on. That might seem obvious now, but it was anything but at the time. Hadoop was starting to explode onto the technical scene 2009. I wouldn't have called it *mainstream* adoption, but it was certainly transitioning from *bleeding*-edge to *leading*-edge uses.

The forming of Explorys coincided with the first Hadoop World conference in October 2009. I was there with about 500 people in the Roosevelt Hotel ballroom in New York City for a one-day conference and it was palpable that something special was happening. People were talking about clusters of a thousand nodes and more – heady stuff. No reasonable software engineer expected any of this to be *easy*, but rather it was about what was *possible*. Somebody from Yahoo did a keynote presentation on how they refactored a search indexing job that used to take three *weeks* to run on in heavily multi-threaded C++ code on a Sun 64-CPU StarFire to a Java MapReduce job that ran in 20 minutes on a 2,000-node cluster. *Twenty Minutes.* He was wearing jeans, polo shirt, and tennis shoes, the uniform of the person who took their code very seriously but their personal appearance much less so. People were standing on their chairs with lighters ablaze in a *Freebird*-encore style, at least mentally. To do so actually would be a bit dangerous as this was only a modestly physically coordinated software engineering crowd, but *mentally* … oh, mentally it was totally happening. This was the future, right here, right now. I also remember someone from IBM doing a keynote presentation, and they must have been an event sponsor to get such a premier spot. He was wearing a suit. He was talking about spreadsheets or something. The contrast from the Yahoo presentation and the IBM presentation could not have been more stark. I remember thinking "What happened to that company? They used to be so innovative."

I managed to track down Christophe Bisciglia, one of the founders of Cloudera, the sponsor and organizer of the conference, and told him about our plans. Mind you Explorys had only been formally incorporated for a couple of *days* at that point. Cloudera was about a 50-person company at the time and was also seeking growth. Explorys wasn't exactly the profile of "enterprise customer" they were seeking to target. We were a startup, and we were in Cleveland, Ohio to boot. Not a place that people normally associate with startups. But we were trying something in healthcare, and Christophe decided right there that he wanted to work with us. We were doing something real, and not just selling ads, he said. He sensed that we would be an interesting big data showcase, and worked out a support agreement that would work with our budget. Kudos to Cloudera for taking the chance, their support was critical.

We immediately set up a consulting day in their Burlingame, California office a few weeks later, which is where I learned about Word-Aligned Hybrid compression.

Everstream

There were reasons I was so excited about the potential of Hadoop and big data frameworks. McHale, Lougheed, and I were all at a company called Everstream before Explorys.

A great deal of the initial technical direction of Explorys was influenced by experiences from Everstream. As of writing (2024), there is a company called "Everstream" that sells business fiber connections, but this is not the same company.

Everstream was a company founded in 1999 in Cleveland, Ohio that was originally a music streaming service, which targeted newspaper websites to place its music (and advert) player. This was *years* before Pandora and Spotify. Everstream might have been *too* far ahead of its time and the company wound up laying off most of its employees around 2002. Everstream wandered around for a while performing odd consulting gigs and eventually found a niche in Video On Demand (VOD) data collection and reporting in early 2004. This is when the only at-home streaming options were through the cable company (e.g., tune to channel 500 for the VOD application). I joined Everstream at this time. Everstream was acquired by Concurrent Computer Corporation in August 2005, and McHale left six months later. Lougheed left about a year and a half after that. Concurrent eventually rebranded Everstream as something else, and then let the Everstream trademark lapse which is how it got reclaimed by another business. I was at Everstream/Concurrent until 2009.

While neither McHale, Lougheed, and I were coming in with any healthcare experience, Everstream brought significant data integration, data management, and product development experiences to the table.

What's in a Name?

Explorys was founded, officially, in October 2009 via a deal with Cleveland Clinic Innovations. The skunkworks started much earlier with a variety of conversations with Cleveland Clinic. I got involved in the Summer of 2009.

Naming a startup is hard. It consists of multiple sessions generating name ideas, and 80% of them will be terrible. Fifteen percent of them will be mediocre. And if you're lucky 4% of them will be decent. And if you're really lucky 1% of them will be good. And not just "good" – but also be trademark, service-mark, and copyright clear, and the domain name will be available. The name *Explorys* came from an ad/marketing person that we were working with. It was a good name.

One of the names I generated that had some traction in the ideation process was VennPoint. Explorys is a much better name than that, but one of the name-*themes* I liked was intersecting sets as it represented the general idea of population exploration. While this particular name-idea wasn't used, the underlying notion wound up in another place: if one looked closely at the Explorys logo it contained three intersecting sets in a Venn diagram.

Chapter 3

Scaling a Startup

One Crazy Year

There is a sweet spot in the balance of intelligence and ignorance: being smart enough to know something is possible, confident enough with one's experiences to accept the challenge, but dumb enough not to be intimidated by the unknown. November 2009 to November 2010 was one of those years.

McHale, Lougheed, and I went to the American Medical Informatics Association (AMIA) Annual Symposium in November 2009 in San Francisco. The Annual Symposium is AMIA's big yearly conference. I was familiar with technical conferences, but this was a different vibe. Attendees at AMIA were generally wearing slacks, dress-shirts, and sports coats. It felt like work. Fancy work. I think it also started on the weekend.

I quickly saw how big but small this sector was. We were watching AMIA's Morris F. Collen award presentation, the organization's lifetime achievement award, when Lougheed chanced to see an opportunity to meet Morris F. Collen himself. Lougheed walked up and made an introduction. Collen

DOI: 10.4324/9781003491590-3

extended his hand to Lougheed in the friendly and confident way of someone who has their name on the award on the podium, smiled, and said, "I don't know you."

Lougheed was in-line with the conference dress code and didn't look materially different from anyone else at the conference, and a small crowd started gathering around him. Collen was a legend, and they saw Collen and Lougheed shaking hands. But they didn't hear what Collen actually said. However, through the transitive property, if Morris F. Collen is speaking to someone in slacks, dress shirt, and sport coat with an AMIA conference badge, then that person was probably worth talking to. Explorys was off to a decent start.

One year later Explorys would return to the AMIA Annual Symposium not just as an attendee but an exhibiter with its first product.

Nouns, Verbs, and Adjectives

Functional domains tend to accrue specific terminologies, and the more complex the domain, the greater the number of words. The financial sector has its vocabulary, and lawyers have another. The military is famous for speaking not just in their own vernacular but in acronyms. Words can bounce from domain to domain as well, such as *socket* being borrowed from electrical engineering to network programming. Healthcare has a sizable vocabulary as well. Efforts to standardize medical terminologies have been around a surprisingly long time, particularly with respect to computerization, and they came in the form of ontologies, taxonomies, and codesets.

One of the most foundational use-cases for medical terminologies is Population Search: to determine how many patients have particular diagnoses or have prescribed a certain medication, for example. In order to effectively answer that question, it must first be agreed those diagnoses and medications are concepts that could be recorded somewhere in the patient's chart or interpreted downstream consistently. And the devil is in the details in terms of which diagnoses and which medications and how they are represented, which is why standardized terminology is so important.

Nearly every healthcare or medical informatics article or book will reference major healthcare terminologies such as SNOMED, RxNorm, and LOINC. But most references will not emphasize just how large these terminologies are. Standardized terminologies are powerful, but their respective sizes can present non-trivial software design challenges.

Work on the Systemized Nomenclature of Medicine, better known as SNOMED, started in 1965 by the College of American Pathologists. SNOMED was overhauled significantly in 2002 when it became SNOMED CT (Clinical Terminology). SNOMED CT is not only large, containing more than 350,000 concepts, but is also complex as it is represented as a Directed Acyclic Graph (DAG). Concepts can have multiple inbound and outbound edges – what the lines-with-arrows that connect concepts are called – as well as multiple edge types. The "Clinical finding (finding)" subgraph alone contains ~120,000 concepts. Examples:

- Metabolic disease (disorder)
- Disorder of endocrine system (disorder)
- Disorder of glucose metabolism (disorder)
- Diabetes mellitus (disorder)

LOINC (Logical Observation Identifiers Names and Codes) was created by Regenstrief Institute in 1994 for the standardization of medical laboratory observations. LOINC currently has over 100,000 concepts, with over 60,000 concepts being lab-related. Examples include:

- Hemoglobin A1c [Mass/volume] in Blood [41995-2]
- Hemoglobin A1c/Hemoglobin.total in Blood [4548-4]

RxNorm is a terminology for medications. Early research for standard medication terminology started in 2001 in Unified Medical Language System (UMLS), and RxNorm began monthly releases in 2005. RxNorm contains at least nine different medication datatypes such as ingredients, precise ingredients, brand names, and clinical drug components. Per the RxNorm release statistics, there are well over 300,000 concepts across the different Term Types. Examples include:

- Ingredient: metformin
- Precise Ingredient: metFORMIN hydrochloride
- Brand Name: Glucophage
- Dose Form Group: metFORMIN Oral Liquid Product

The eResearch proposal mentioned SNOMED as something that *could* be utilized, but eResearch didn't attempt to do anything with it. Simply knowing about SNOMED, however, wasn't the hard part as it was a frequent mention for research analytics that I saw myself at the AMIA Annual Symposium in November 2009. The hard part was *doing* something with it, in a product, that could be used effectively.

For Explorys' desired version of population searching even if we just used *some* of SNOMED, such as the Clinical Findings and Procedure sub-graphs that are around 160,000 concepts. Add in LOINC, RxNorm, and other codesets such as ICD-9 and CPT and the number starts to conservatively approach *500,000* concepts for starters. That is already *multiple hundreds of times* more concepts than eResearch ever supported, and it would only continue to grow over time. By the time those concepts were split into multiple time-buckets (e.g., "ever," "last year," "last 3 years"), we could easily wind up with over *1.5 million* "searchable bits" per patient.

For starters.

It was clear that Explorys' Population Search solution was going to require very different approach than eResearch. No code from eResearch was ever used in any Explorys solution.

Everstream Influences

Everstream had a number of challenges that were relevant to Explorys specifically and to big data in general, including but not limited to distributed data collection, data warehousing, data standardization, software product development, software sales and support. Everstream had pushed the technology that was commercially available at the time, including Oracle, with significant workloads that taught much about the limits of single server architectures. Everstream provided years of experiences with respect to what was possible with existing architecture, what was difficult, and what it took to operate it. Everstream provided years of patterns and – just as importantly – *anti*-patterns when I started Explorys engineering in 2009.

Hosted

I had enough experience for a lifetime supporting on-premise deployments at Everstream. Because Everstream's solutions was deployed in the customer environment, we typically had little insight into the performance until something went wrong. Then we were on the phone under emergency conditions, and entirely on our heels. It's a tough way to live, and I didn't want to see it repeated with Explorys.

While it was going to take great software engineering to make Explorys successful, we weren't going to be selling technology per se – we needed to be selling successful *solutions*. This was a significant product decision. I didn't make this decision alone, but this decision sure as heck didn't happen without me.

While being cloud-based is obvious *now*, it was much less obvious to the market in 2009. Healthcare organizations were *extremely* suspicious of public cloud vendors in 2009; so Explorys utilized Expedient, a commercial hosting provider, which had a Cleveland data center. Explorys was a "cloud" as far as our customers were concerned. Self-hosting was important because Explorys not only needed to be able to move fast, but we needed the flexibility to adapt and evolve our technical stack behind-the-scenes. Explorys needed to control its own environment to do that.

Distributed Data Collection

Everstream had data collection software called the IDG (Interactive Data Gateway). Cable companies wanted an enterprise view of their video on demand services, but the service delivery platforms were deployed at a market level at that time due to technical capabilities of the day. Larger customers could have *dozens* of markets. Everstream provided many useful experiences in distributed data collection.

One of the unfortunate experiences is that Everstream would provide its customers a device specification for the IDG software, but they would purchase machines with half the storage and compute necessary. Because IDGs were needed on a per-market basis, this was an attempt at penny-pinching. But when the IDGs got over-loaded or run out of space then Everstream would be the last to know because it wasn't our hardware, but it was still our fault as it was "our software." Painful to support at the time, but a good lesson.

Explorys needed data collection software too. For starters, Explorys borrowed the name of collector, changed a letter, and called it the HDG (Health Data Gateway). Now it was a whole new thing. Presto!

The entire data collection stack was re-written using Apache ActiveMQ for store and forward messaging, and it was deployed in a rackable server with a configuration of our own specification, including security. This wasn't just data collection software, it was a data collection *appliance*. And it was included in the price of the solution. If the component appliance ever failed, it was on us to replace it. But that was perfectly fine by engineering, because we could manage it.

Open Source

Where possible, I wanted to leverage open-source software at Explorys.

Everstream leveraged Oracle's database both inside the IDG software, as well as for the data warehousing product it sold. Oracle tends to be on the pricey side, especially for enterprise features like table partitioning. All major database platforms have idiosyncrasies that emerge at scale, but Oracle generally worked pretty well. My concerns were more on the business end as Everstream was using Oracle's OEM (Original Equipment Manufacturer) pricing for the IDG, which had some technical and contractual requirements. Oracle can be "enthusiastic" to put it mildly about patrolling its contracts, which can make life interesting. A few audits can start to make a person start thinking very carefully about technical dependencies and business partners.

Consequently, I was leery about our fate being in a single vendor's hands.

Horizontal Scalability

Everstream's data warehousing product was Oracle-based, which was typical of solutions during the period, and was often co-deployed on a sizable database server, which was also typical of deployments at the time, with other non-Everstream solutions. As Everstream was just selling software, it wasn't in much of a position to demand a separate environment.

What we often found is no matter how big the server was, there was always an inevitable clash over resources between the deployed applications. We frequently hit "scale up" limits. I half-jokingly called this "The 49th Processor Problem" based on actual customer experiences. When a database running on a 48-CPU SuperDome is tapped out and 100% utilized, where do you go from there? 48 CPUs was a lot of computing power back in the day, and arguably still is. Unfortunately, if the solution is designed for a single server, the answer is *nowhere*. You are stuck.

Consequently, I wanted to be able to scale horizontally where-ever possible. And that also required controlling the environment.

Data Source Management

In addition to multiple markets, there were multiple source systems per market. For example, for a single market there could be a streaming platform, a billing/back-office platform, and sometimes a different media asset management platform. There was also typically another feed for provisioned settops and the associated subscriber. All these data sources had to be merged together for a coherent picture. This also raised the question of how to transform all this data into a common model, and still know where all the data came from.

Population Explorer

Explorys' first solution was a Population Search application called "Population Explorer." It was later renamed "Explore" and then had a further rename to "Cohort Discovery" under

IBM. Most Explorys engineers will remember it by its nickname "PopEx."

Given the design goal of term searching, it became clear we couldn't just have a dropdown of 500,000 concepts or more like eResearch had. Even splitting it up into multiple drop-downs was still unwieldy. Few analytic products utilized SNOMED and LOINC as they were primarily viewed as research frameworks at the time. Real healthcare analytics used ICD and CPT codes. Even analysts at Cleveland Clinic told us that.

Google was already firmly established by 2009, and so high-quality freetext searches that are fast were already something people were getting used to. A Cloudera engineer who had interned at Google once told me about Google Search "they have way more servers than you think they do, and everything is in memory." That was a humorous oversimplification, of course, but it is also an acknowledgment of the difficulty of the problem and for how Google made it look easy. Delivering high-quality freetext searches over large amounts of data that are also fast is a hard problem. A very hard problem.

I came up with the design compromise approach of walking the user into target terminologies that the application supported. We weren't going to support truly freetext searches over the underlying data, but we would still support freetext searching over multiple hundreds of supported terminology concepts. Population Explorer also supported *type-ahead* search, where the search terms were updated with each additional keystroke. Back in 2009–2010, that wasn't common in most web applications.

Due to copyright permissions, I was unable to use images of Population Explore, but I can still describe it.

There were three visual sections of the Fast Search user interface:

Terminology Search – was a Google-like search capability for criteria that could be added to a search Cohort.

Searches could be targeted an "organization" (e.g., the user's own healthcare organization, the Universe, or a licensed Therapeutic Dataset) and had a datatype selector (e.g., diagnosis, medication, observation).

Cohort – Search qualifier, including "not" option as well as and/or options between criterion. There was also the capability to convert to a Fast Search cohort definition to a PowerSearch.

Browse – Browse The Crowd was the piece de resistance of Population Explorer. This described the characteristics of a search result, across datatypes such as diagnoses, observations, medications, procedures, and vitals.

Another search issue that I had to address was search term response. Not just that it comes back fast, but what is being returned. Consider the following SNOMED terms, which should be returned first, second, and third if a user types in "diabetes"

- "Atypical diabetes mellitus"
- "Diabetes mellitus"
- "Diabetes mellitus type 1"
- "Diabetes mellitus type 2"
- "Fulminant type 1 diabetes mellitus"

A straightforward solution would be to return them in alphabetical order. But effective search is about *relevance* of response. Population Explorer was using Apache Lucene for terminology searches and configuring the appropriate "boosting" – how Lucene refers to the ranking of responses – took a lot of trial and error. I wrote an algorithm to calculate the number of descendants each term had to determine just how "high" – so to speak – the concept was in the graph. I had optimized Population Search for more general terms to show up first, so users could get a broader sense of a population and then allowing them to drill-in to more specific terms.

An example of Fast Search term-search results with boosting when searching on "diabetes" would be as follows:

Diagnosis: Diabetes Mellitus
Diagnosis: Lipoatrophic diabetes
Diagnosis: Diabetes insipidus
Diagnosis: Nephrogenic diabetes insipidus
Finding: Brittle diabetes mellitus
Diagnosis: Gestational diabetes mellitus
Diagnosis: History of diabetes mellitus
Diagnosis: Hypoglycemic event in diabetes
Diagnosis: Fibrocalculous pancreatic diabetes

To further aid in usability, search terms that had no patients were italicized ("Lipoatrophic diabetes" in the example above), providing immediate and guiding visual feedback. While Population Explorer patient searching was internally based on compressed bitsets, there was a significant amount of code like this for metadata management on the backend and metadata navigation in the application that made all of this come together as a solution.

Population Explorer also underwent a process for statistical de-identification through Expert Determination. The counts were all blurred to the nearest ten, and the search time-periods wouldn't go less than one year, for example. Again, this was all net-new functionality as eResearch didn't have such certification.

PowerSearch was another search feature in Population Explorer that was entirely made possible by the Hadoop infrastructure. Users could visually define complex queries with custom ranges and event sequencing (e.g., "patients prescribed medication X with lab-test Y results dropping by 10% within 6 months") and then they would run on the grid. Some searches might take a few minutes, and some might take many minutes. Although we aimed to continually make things faster,

PowerSearch was a Dancing Elephant situation: it was amazing that any of this was a reality. PowerSearch allowed an iterative searching over a scale of patient data and query complexity that wasn't previously possible. Population Explore users would typically do quick-and-dirty patient count assessments in FastSearch and then do further refinements in PowerSearch. It was a powerful one-two punch.

Naturally, there also was an office move in the middle of this development, but we'll get back to that later.

Building the Team

Although the Explorys story runs from 2009 to 2018 it already can sound like a modern anachronism in the post-Covid-19-pandemic era. The entire engineering staff was not only co-located in Cleveland, it was also working largely in-person. Now this probably sounds as out of place as sharing 6-Sigma engineering stories from a buggy-whip factory, but the experiences are worth recounting because effective teams are not easy to build, and they take time to form. And Explorys built a terrifically talented engineering team. These are practices that should never go out of style.

When Explorys was founded, it was suggested that we should recruit at MIT (Massachusetts Institute of Technology), as MIT is a famous university with strong technical programs. It is no doubt an aspirational recruiting location. I replied that I would be happy to interview anyone interested in working at Explorys, including MIT students, but the question with recruiting is who do you – for lack of a better word – *chase*?

As MIT is in Boston, the logistics were not hypothetical to me as my brother-in-law lived there. It's a 10-to-12 hour drive each way from Cleveland, with travel time dictated by how many screaming children or executives are in the car. That is two days right there. The career fair would be another day.

And when driving that far you might as well tack on another day for follow-up interviews the next day. The single-day career fair has now consumed most of the work week, and for multiple people as sending a single individual to staff a booth is neither effective nor a great look. One could speed things up with air-travel, of course. But it would still be advisable to come in the night before, and flying introduces new logistical issues for transporting supplies. When driving the display and career fair handouts could be packed in the trunk. Those supplies might have to be either packed or shipped, and Explorys would have minimal to no support staff. All that extra logistics coordination was going to fall on the people attending the career fair, like me, not executive leadership. These are the details that make recruiting successful. And I'm not professional recruiter, just software engineer that wants to have effective recruiting.

Then, after all that, we needed to convince people not just to work for Explorys but to move to Cleveland. All that effort for one college. If Billy Beane was looking for software engineers rather than baseball players, these are some of the questions he would ask.

There was an underlying assumption of *transactionality* in the suggestion as well. It's true in a sense, of course, because college recruiting is basically shopping for students, but when companies only show up on campus for career fairs and are otherwise unresponsive, it is a bit one-sided. Worse, when companies only show up every couple of years and then they expect colleges to be at their beck and call to deliver students like some sort of higher-education concierge. Career center staffers don't love that and neither does the academic staff.

I thought we should do better. I wanted to build recruiting *relationships* – Explorys needed to be supporting full-time recruitment and intern recruitment, year over year. We needed to be showing up doing talks to student groups, where possible guest talks, and most importantly talk about interesting topics – not just typical recruitment sales pitches, and I led these efforts. We needed to own our own backyard, and I defined that as a three-hour driving radius around Cleveland as that was about the limit for an out-and-back for a recruiting fair in a single day. Realistically maybe 2.5 hours, but three hours tops. Explorys was a career center partner with Case Western Reserve University, which was a mile away from Explorys, and I did a number of talks to the Hacker's Society, computer science student group. Explorys also established a close relationship with Kent State University, about 45 minutes south, as I did a number of guest talks there as well. Explorys sponsored hackathons both at Case and Kent State and hired a number of students from both colleges. Explorys also made regular appearances to Carnegie Mellon University in the early days, and there were periodic trips to University of Pittsburgh, Ohio State University, University of Michigan as well.

This was all a lot of work, but it was worth it.

Early career recruiting, as important as that was, was just one part of a larger effort. The Cleveland Big Data Meetup represented a forum to showcase work as well as foster professional networking in the region.

AMIA 2010

The AMIA Annual Symposium took place in November 2010 in Washington, DC. Explorys had an exhibitor booth, its first solution, the Population Explorer application, and multiple integrated healthcare systems as customers. A humble position given where Explorys would be in a few years, but astonishing progress from the year before. I alternated between attending sessions when I could and giving demos at the booth.

When AMIA ended, we saw all the exhibitors packing up their small items, shaking hands, and walking out. That is, everybody except myself and another Explorys staff

Figure 3.1 **Explorys at a Case Western Reserve University recruiting fair (2011).**

Figure 3.2 **Case alumni at Explorys. Courtesy of the Case Alumni Association. This picture appeared in a CAA magazine in 2018. As big as this group was, it was still missing a few people.**

Figure 3.3 Explorys engineers at a Cleveland Big Data Mega Meetup (2014).

member. Because the new Explorys display cost something like $12,000, McHale and Lougheed decided that it would be wise to save money and not pay for the conference logistics staff who were now streaming in and starting to tear down and pack up displays. McHale and Lougheed needed to attend an important business dinner, they explained. I was needed to break down and pack up the display. And don't scratch anything because the new display cost $12,000, I was reminded.

Everybody else on the floor at this point was dressed like a concert roadie – jeans, boots, t-shirt, and a well-worn hoodie – and I was still wearing when I was giving demos at the display to conference attendees a few hours earlier. So, along with another co-worker, we spent the next two hours carefully breaking down and packing the display on a pallet, ready for shipping. Explorys was the *only* company at AMIA breaking down its own display. Whatever it takes, I guess. I would

Figure 3.4 American Medical Informatics Association (AMIA) Annual Symposium 2010.

Figure 3.5 AMIA Annual Symposium 2010 – display breakdown. I was not thrilled.

have liked to have seen just how much money Explorys saved, though.

For some reason I agreed to break down the display next year at the 2011 AMIA Annual Symposium as well because I was a team player and what not. But that was my last breakdown, I insisted. It was time to hire roadies.

More of Whatever It Takes

2010 ended with one of my favorite customer quotes: "they are coachable."

It was a "mostly-complement", and it was at least in part referring to me. One of the Cleveland Clinic research coordinators that I had been working with to review the development progress of Population Explorer did a reference call in the Fall of 2010 for another healthcare organization about

Explorys. She was trying to describe Explorys' relative inexperience in healthcare but also our willingness to do whatever it took to produce results. And we would listen – not a trait always found in healthcare.

That prospective customer did end up signing with Explorys, so the reference must have worked. Or at least didn't hurt. Saying that we were coachable wasn't exactly the most glowing review, but considering where Explorys was a year prior, I'll take it.

Healthcare's Worst Kept Secret: Secondary Use

There were various phrases in the tech industry at the time such as "data is the new oil" and "digital exhaust." The former I don't remember hearing at Explorys, which I was glad because the *old* oil has hardly been a recipe for stability and peace around the world. But the latter unfortunately was. I hated that phrase. Exhaust is what comes from tailpipes. Exhaust kills. That wasn't supposed to be our brand.

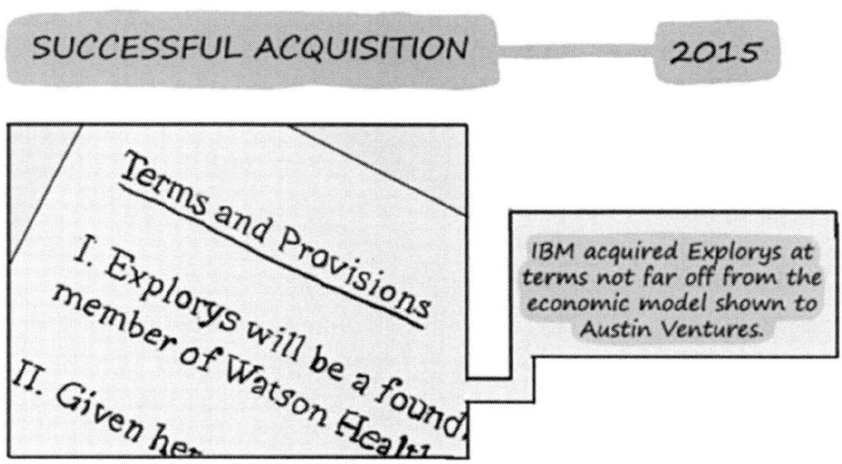

Figure 3.6 Explorys Graphic Corporate History by Braun Ink (2015).

When venture capitalists referred to Explorys' economic model, it was fundamentally about the value of patient data. That is crass when you think about it, but healthcare allows for this via its Secondary Use provision in HIPAA. It's illegal, of course, to sell Protected Health Information (PHI), and HIPAA makes that clear. But de-identified data is a different story. That is what Secondary Use is all about. It is effectively digital exhaust.

Explorys leveraged this to serve both healthcare organizations, as well as pharmaceutical and life science customers via HIPAA's Secondary Use provision. An overwhelming number of healthcare tech companies are either doing this or trying to do this, sometimes viewing the Provider sector as a "cost of doing business" in order to get data to sell it to the Life Science and Pharmaceutical sectors.

Crass, I know.

Most healthcare tech companies will sell Secondary Use data sets, and then Life Science and Pharmaceutical companies would combine them with other acquired datasets as input for their analytic efforts. Secondary Use states that the de-identification risk needs to be *low*, but it's not *zero*. The more datasets are floating around, the greater the risk that someone will re-identify the patient either accidentally or on purpose.

Explorys received Secondary Use access to healthcare data from the Data Use Agreements that it had with its healthcare customers, and that data could be added to *The Universe*, which is what Explorys called its de-identified Secondary Use dataset. Most healthcare customers granted Explorys these data rights in exchange for access to search the Universe in Population Explorer to support their own research efforts. The intention was to provide benefit to all parties involved, and not just about extracting dollars from data.

Explorys also took a different technical approach to Secondary Use by leasing access to datasets in the Explorys hosted environment, and datasets didn't leave that environment. This pattern of data access caused a few grumbles for Life Science and Pharma analysts, but it represented a reasonable and effective compromise between data access and security. I thought this approach had the best interests of patients and healthcare data safety in mind.

Products and Teams

Explorys had solutions for both healthcare providers as well as Secondary Use sectors, and one of the reasons why Explorys was effective was its unified architecture and data pipeline. Data sources could be ingested and prepared once but utilized for multiple applications downstream. This approach is easy to say, but not an easy thing to *do* from an engineering standpoint.

The Healthcare Provider sector was served through multiple products. The Population Explorer application could be used for fast slicing and dicing on their own organization, as well as the de-identified Universe. Enterprise Performance Manager (EPM) was a suite of functionality for clinical measures, registries, and a Virtual Chart to view patient data across multiple sources. SuperMart-Provider was a hosted data warehouse with all of the above information. An API tier was also added in 2017/2018.

The Secondary Use sector was served through the Population Explorer application, where Life Science and Pharmaceutical researchers could search on the de-identified Universe, and also license access to Therapeutic Data Sets served out of SuperMart-SecondaryUse. In the National Institutes of Health (NIH) PubMed database, there are over 200 references to Explorys, the Explore/Cohort Discovery application, and Explorys' Therapeutic Datasets as a key data source, which is no small feat.

There were multiple engineering teams that made all of that happen. The Applications team developed Population Explorer and EPM applications. The Continuous Integration/Continuous Deployment (CI/CD) team managed the build environments and supported the automated deployment of releases. The SuperMart team managed both SuperMart deployments (Provider and Secondary Use). The Engines team developed the Measure Engine, the registry engine, and the attribution engine. The indexing team managed the core data pipeline for data preparation of patient matching, applying configured standardization, running configured derived record handlers, and configured risk models. When things broke in the middle of the night, unfortunately, it was the indexing team that had to dig in, and it was not-infrequently an exotic data situation. The Data Acquisition team developed the data acquisition frameworks that the services teams utilized, including the HDG collection framework as well as transformation frameworks. The DevOps team managed all the data center infrastructure, including racking and stacking of over a thousand servers, automated monitoring and patching, and the high-end networking that was required for performant clusters, as well as the thankless job of IT support for employee laptops and office. And speaking of thankless jobs, there was the application QA team.

In addition to engineering, the Analytics team produced productized measures and registries that could be used out of the box and implemented dozens of risk models. And the Services team was essential for customer onboarding with a METL (record mapping and ETL) team that managed data transformation from source format to the Explorys internal data model, a Standardization team that managed standardization of dozens of attributes per source to Explorys-supported ontologies, taxonomies, and codesets. Plus, the Services team handled customizations of measures and registries as needed.

It took multiple teams and a lot of people to make Explorys happen.

Figure 3.7 Early Explorys engineers 2011.

Figure 3.8 Explorys in May 2011 at its second office (GCIC).

Community

Explorys greatly benefited from the big data technical community, which was not just *open* from the perspective of open-source codebases, but also open in sharing experiences. It was hard work operating at scale.

I contributed my first patch to the Apache HBase community in late 2010 and a couple dozen patches later, I was voted a *committer* by the rest of the Apache HBase team. A committer is someone entrusted to make direct changes to the codebase. My contributions to HBase were centered around improving the documentation in the online HBase Reference Guide and assisting other users in the forums. This represented my nights and weekend work. I wasn't getting paid for any of this, but it helped HBase become a better framework, and since Explorys was utilizing HBase, it also helped Explorys in multiple ways, such as improving the documentation that all early-stage frameworks sorely need but usually lack. It also built credibility and trust with other community members. And the occasional favor.

One of those favors was when HBase project lead Michael Stack flew out to visit us one weekend and review our deployment. Explorys paid for his ticket and hotel, of course, but he did this for Explorys because of the community connection. He did that on his own personal time because he could see we were committed to making HBase successful, we were doing something interesting in big data (healthcare) and were likable for the most part. Or at least not obnoxious. Whatever it takes.

Forward Motion

There is a balance between building for extensibility and scalability, and overdoing it and over-complicating the design. One of my favorite YouTube talks on software engineering is

Figure 3.9 Michael Stack, project manager of the Apache HBase project, visits Explorys (Early 2011).

Figure 3.10 Author with Doug Cutting, co-creator of Hadoop. The big data framework was named for his child's stuffed elephant, which his son named "Hadoop." This is why the mascot of Hadoop became the yellow elephant.

Figure 3.11 Author with Christophe Bisciglia from Cloudera (2012).

Figure 3.12 Explorys at HBaseCon (2012). Todd Lipcon at left.

"Building Software Systems at Google and Lessons Learned" by Jeff Dean from November 2010, where he walked through 11 years of experiences in building Google Search. Dean was a co-author of Google's MapReduce and Bigtable papers, among many other accomplishments, and was named an

Figure 3.13 Author at HBaseCon 2013.

Association for Computing Machinery (ACM) Fellow, among other honorifics. Per the talk, Google Search had "7 significant revisions" between 1999 and 2010, which I would interpret as "major releases," as well as countless minor releases. The reason was that Google processed about 1,000 times more documents from 1999 to 2010, handled 1,000 times greater query volume, reduced the query latency, and changed the update frequency of the search index from monthly to sub-minute. And it wasn't just the software that was getting updated: infrastructure capacity increased 1,000 times with more and faster servers. Even someone as smart as Jeff Dean couldn't anticipate *everything*. The main theme of the talk was to keep learning, adapting, and moving forward. Words to live by in software engineering that sound simple but aren't always so easy to put into practice.

In that vein, there are few decisions that I'd like to take back from Explorys. Such is life. I wrote a post for the Association for Computing Machinery called "Software Learning: The Art of Design Regret" on the challenges of

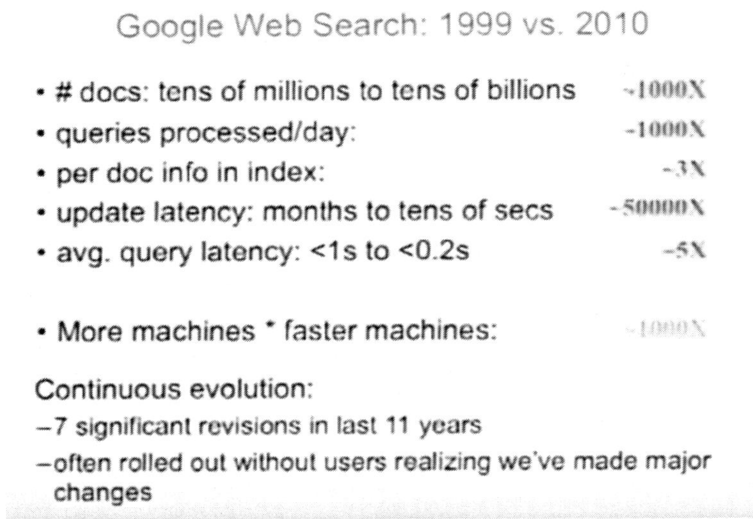

Figure 3.14 Slide from "Building Software Systems at Google and Lessons Learned." https://www.youtube.com/watch?v=modXC5IWTJI

decision-making. Sometimes mistakes happen. More often, there are unknown consequences that seem reasonable at the time, especially in a fast-changing environment. There are missed opportunities, and those can sting. And there is also anachronistic regret, where people beat themselves up over options that weren't actually feasible at the time. Most importantly, there are tradeoffs in any technical decision. Explorys engineering put a priority on performance, data completeness, and data quality for the portfolio of solutions. As the technical stack was built on multiple emerging frameworks, the technical stack was non-trivial and required a lot from engineers. The platform was powerful, but it wasn't always the easiest to navigate when seen from the inside out. Overall, though, Explorys was able to select a number of significant technical patterns that proved effective and was able to keep most mistakes small, avoiding anything fatal. Explorys kept moving forward, making the best decisions possible with the information available at the time.

Explorys Messaging

Early press releases and stories about Explorys had explicit mentions of the Cleveland Clinic collaboration, a big part of the origin story as it gave Explorys credibility in healthcare. Everstream, even as late as 2011, was also an explicit mention if the stories didn't mention the Everstream influence on Explorys engineering.

> Lougheed and McHale sold the previous company they founded, Everstream, for $15 million to Concurrent Computer in 2005. Everstream sold software that provided video-on-demand reporting, analytics and statistics.
>
> **Med City News (May 2011)**

What was *not* mentioned in the early years was that Explorys was built on "Cleveland Clinic technology." That message started after Dr Jain joined in late Summer 2011, almost two years after founding, and then the messaging became bifurcated. Big Data had become an extremely hot topic not just in healthcare but in every sector by that time. Demonstrating tech credibility to customers was critical, and this required a different technical origin story. Explorys strongly promoted its use of big data frameworks in customer presentations.

This is the way the Explorys platform was described in a customer-facing slide circa 2012, for example:

- System Connectors:
  - Clinical systems
  - Operational systems
  - Financial systems
- Big Data Engines:
  - Curation Engine
  - Attribution Engine

  - Master Patient Index
  - Measure and Registry Engine
  - Analytics and Reports Engine
  - Data Governance Engine
- Services and Applications:
  - Informatics reports and analytics
  - EPM: Explore
  - EPM: Measure
  - EPM: Registry
  - EPM: Engage
  - Third Party Applications
  - Third Party Reports and BI Tools
- Big Data Storage
  - (with a graphic of a cluster of machines, and caption "massively parallel processing")
  - Hadoop logo
  - HBase logo

Big Data and Hadoop were very much front and center, both in reality in the architecture as well as when described to customers. Explorys PDFs from early 2013 that have similar content can be found on the Internet Archive's Wayback Machine:

- https://web.archive.org/web/20130412210515/https://www.explorys.com/docs/data-sheets/explorys-overview.pdf
- https://web.archive.org/web/20130412221434/https://www.explorys.com/docs/data-sheets/epm-explore---fact-sheet.pdf

A slide that was frequently used in the Explorys technical overview deck emphasized Explorys' involvement in the big data community. It was a screenshot of the Apache HBase list of committers, a distributed key-value framework inspired by the Google Bigtable paper, which Explorys was utilizing for record storage.

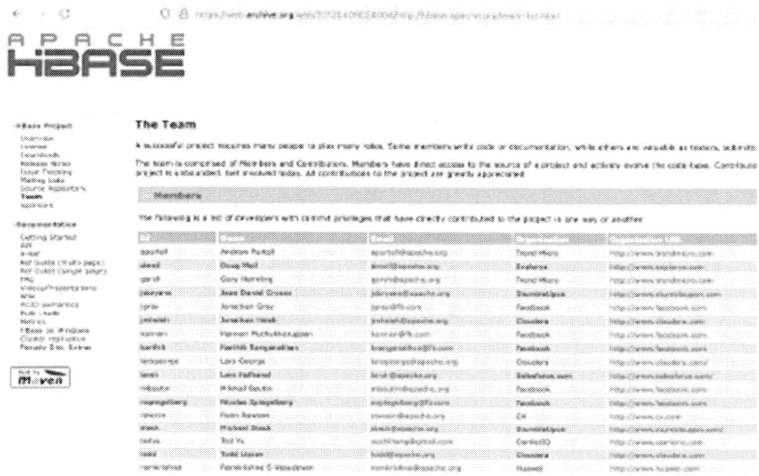

Figure 3.15 Apache HBase committers (early 2012): https://web.archive.org/web/20120409024004/http://hbase.apache.org/team-list.html

While I could not include the original slide for copyright reasons, one can get the general idea of what this slide looked like by looking again at the Internet Archive's Wayback Machine. Look at the Apache HBase committer list below and imagine a large callout text box stating "Explorys Leads Healthcare BIG DATA" with an arrow pointing to "Explorys" in the organization column.

While I *am* very proud of Explorys leading healthcare big data, the fact that it was my name two columns over was not a part of the story, though. It was one message for customers, and another for the press.

"and the three men brought Explorys to life."

Explorys Ascending

The Pivot

Explorys demonstrated the importance of being flexible and adaptive. From its inception in 2009 to roughly the Summer of 2011, Explorys was focused on serving the research sector through Population Explorer. Healthcare organizations could search on their data for free as well as get access to search on the Universe. Life Science and Pharmaceutical companies paid for access to search on the Universe through Population Explorer. But although Explorys was growing, it was also clear that this path was a bit too narrow. Explorys decided to develop a suite of provider sector functionality through the Enterprise Performance Manager (EPM) suite and actually stopped taking new Secondary Use customers. It was a bold move. Initial work on EPM:Measure started in the Summer of 2011, and the first release of EPM:Measure came out in the Fall. The first version of EPM:Registry released in mid-December 2011. I remember this well because I was working through the company Christmas party with a handful of developers until midnight getting it stabilized.

Clinical Measures sound simple in concept: numerator over denominator, and the units can be things like patients or events. But a quick look at a fairly straightforward measure (NQF 0059: Diabetes: Hemoglobin A1c (HbA1c) Poor Control (>9%)) illustrates the complexities of their definition. The example below only cites ICD10 codes, for example, for the denominator, and even that list of codes is sizable, and that is only the diagnosis datatype. One could also cite medications indicative of diabetes as well, which would generate an even longer list of inclusion codes, or a clinical observation that is indicative of diabetes. Inclusion criteria can get complicated in a hurry.

Codes are just the beginning; measurement periods are another. NQF 0059 only has one measurement period, but some clinical measures can have multiple, with conditions that must be satisfied within the period or before the period, or even one condition happening before another condition, as well as event specification (e.g., "most recent A1c level") and event counts (e.g., two or more instances), and so on. There are edge cases galore.

DENOMINATOR:
Patients 18 - 75 years of age with diabetes with a visit during the measurement period

Denominator Criteria (Eligible Cases):
Patients 18 through 75 years of age on date of encounter
AND
Diagnosis for diabetes (ICD-10-CM): E10.10, E10.11, E10.21, E10.22, E10.29, E10.311, E10.319, E10.3211, E10.3212, E10.3213, E10.3219, E10.3291, E10.3292, E10.3293, E10.3299, E10.3311, E10.3312, E10.3313, E10.3319, E10.3391, E10.3392, E10.3393, E10.3399, E10.3411, E10.3412, E10.3413, E10.3419, E10.3491, E10.3492, E10.3493, E10.3499, E10.3511, E10.3512, E10.3513, E10.3519, E10.3521, E10.3522, E10.3523, E10.3529, E10.3531, E10.3532, E10.3533, E10.3539, E10.3541, E10.3542, E10.3543, E10.3549, E10.3551, E10.3552, E10.3553, E10.3559, E10.3591, E10.3592, E10.3593, E10.3599, E10.36, E10.37X1, E10.37X2, E10.37X3, E10.37X9, E10.39, E10.40, E10.41, E10.42, E10.43, E10.44, E10.49, E10.51, E10.52, E10.59, E10.610, E10.618, E10.620, E10.621, E10.622, E10.628, E10.630, E10.638, E10.641, E10.649, E10.65, E10.69, E10.8, E10.9, E11.00, E11.01, E11.21, E11.22, E11.29, E11.311, E11.319, E11.3211, E11.3212, E11.3213, E11.3219, E11.3291, E11.3292, E11.3293, E11.3299, E11.3311, E11.3312, E11.3313, E11.3319, E11.3391, E11.3392, E11.3393, E11.3399, E11.3411, E11.3412, E11.3413, E11.3419, E11.3491, E11.3492, E11.3493, E11.3499, E11.3511, E11.3512, E11.3513, E11.3519, E11.3521, E11.3522, E11.3523, E11.3529, E11.3531, E11.3532, E11.3533, E11.3539, E11.3541, E11.3542, E11.3543, E11.3549, E11.3551, E11.3552, E11.3553, E11.3559, E11.3591, E11.3592, E11.3593, E11.3599, E11.36, E11.37X1, E11.37X2, E11.37X3, E11.37X9, E11.39, E11.40, E11.41, E11.42, E11.43, E11.44, E11.49, E11.51, E11.52, E11.59,

Figure 3.16 Denominator of Clinical Measure NQF 59. https://qpp.cms.gov/docs/QPP_quality_measure_specifications/CQM-Measures/2019_Measure_001_MIPSCQM.pdf

NUMERATOR:
Patients whose most recent HbA1c level (performed during the measurement period) is > 9.0%

Numerator Instructions:
INVERSE MEASURE - A lower calculated performance rate for this measure indicates better clinical care or control. The "Performance Not Met" numerator option for this measure is the representation of the better clinical quality or control. Submitting that numerator option will produce a performance rate that trends closer to 0%, as quality increases. For inverse measures, a rate of 100% means all of the denominator eligible patients did not receive the appropriate care or were not in proper control. Patient is numerator compliant if most recent HbA1c level >9% or is missing a result or if an HbA1c test was not done during the measurement year. Ranges and thresholds do not meet criteria for this indicator. A distinct numeric result is required for numerator compliance.

Numerator Options:

	Performance Met:	Most recent hemoglobin A1c level > 9.0% **(3046F)**
	OR	
	Performance Met:	Hemoglobin A1c level was not performed during the measurement period (12 months) **(3046F *with* 8P)**
OR		
	Performance Not Met:	Most recent hemoglobin A1c (HbA1c) level < 7.0% **(3044F)**
	OR	
	Performance Not Met:	Most recent hemoglobin A1c (HbA1c) level 7.0 to 9.0% **(3045F)**

Figure 3.17 Numerator of Clinical Measure NQF 59.

All of this logic had to be specified somewhere, which is why Measure Definition Language (MDL) was created. It was an XML specification of logic and codes that could be configured by a clinical content team. Having a clinical content team working directly in XML wasn't an ideal experience, but it still provided a critical layer of separation from content and engineering teams. Even if Explorys had created a visual tool specifying measure definitions, we still would have had to create MDL anyway as something that the visual tool generated. And under the circumstances, we had to dedicate engineering resources to build the EPM:Measure application, and there were third party XML editors that were available. It's all about tradeoffs.

The Measure Engine took the configured MDLs per healthcare customer and calculated the results, but on top of the common data pipeline's patient-matched, standardized, and augmented prepared dataset. All of this was running at scale on Hadoop.

Another important piece to this puzzle was the provider attribution, which is determining which provider is responsible for a particular patient/measure result. Attribution Definition Language (ADL) was created to complement MDL configuration, as the result could be calculated (e.g., the most number of encounters for a configured specialty) or assigned through an attribution list.

Finally, there was the required configuration of an org-chart to view the summarized results. But org-charts could be seen through multiple perspectives, such as physical location or specialty. As a result, Explorys wound up supporting multiple org-chart options to view summarized results. Kudos to the product teams for the flexibility, but also to the services teams for the follow-through as org-charts often became bespoke activities per customer.

EPM:Measure users might see it as "just a scorecard of clinical measures," which was true enough but also a severe oversimplification. There was so much happening under the hood.

EPM:Registry was a module that presented an analytic view of the same underlying patient data, with one row per patient but with a wide number of calculated data features (columns). Registries could be defined and configured with population inclusion criteria (just like MDL), but then also have logic within data feature definitions. Registries were defined in Registry Definition Language (RDL), which was also XML-based.

Take for example the following registry data features:

- Patient first name
- Patient last name
- Next encounter date
- Diabetes (true/false)
- Last A1c value
- Last A1c date
- Hypertension (true/false)
- Last BP/Systolic value
- Last BP/Systolic date
- Last BP/Diastolic value
- Last BP/Diastolic date

The "Diabetes" and "Hypertension" features above would calculate either "TRUE" or "FALSE," but could each have logic that is as complex as a clinical measure, specifying criteria that spans multiple datatypes such as diagnoses, medications, observations, procedures, or more. And as with clinical measure calculations, the registry calculations ran at scale on Hadoop.

EPM:Measure and EPM:Registry applications allowed users to drill into a patient's Virtual Chart as well, and there were years of enhancements and improvements after the initial release as all users want to find precisely the one thing they are looking for, and quickly, which isn't easy as healthcare data is voluminous and complex. Back-end EPM functionality for measure and registry calculations continued to expand as well. EPM became Explorys' foundation for serving the provider sector. Given that the provider sector was the foundation of the business model, EPM in a very real way became the foundation of Explorys.

An EPM overview PDF can be found on the Internet Archive Wayback Machine from early 2013 here:

https://web.archive.org/web/20130413033820/https://www.explorys.com/docs/data-sheets/epm-measure---fact-sheet.pdf

Data

To support EPM, we needed to overhaul and expand data ingestion. In terms of Data Sources, Explorys would eventually ingest data from Enterprise EHRs (Epic, Cerner, Allscripts, etc.), small practice systems, and a myriad of Files (flat, X12 billing, CDA, HL7, CMS/CCLF, etc.), and over 400 data sources. Datatypes included all the usual health data model suspects, such as demographics, encounter, diagnoses, procedures, medications, observations, lab reports, progress notes, etc.

But it wasn't just about "more data" but more very specific types of data. Group Lists and Eligibility files were ingested to support custom patient-provider attribution. External measure result ingestion was supported in case customers wanted EPM to be aware of calculations happening external to EPM. And a great deal of time was spent ingesting Org-Chart data, obtaining which was a lot harder than one would think.

Checkpoints

When Explorys was raising funds in 2012 we had a consultant come in to review our technical architecture. The consultant was a Google software engineer by day and was moonlighting for Austin Ventures who was leading the prospective round. Overall, he seemed satisfied. Obviously, Explorys wasn't Google-sized, but the technologies Explorys had chosen and implemented and our determination to learn from the best practices of the big data community were noted. One of the key pieces of feedback was for us to keep an eye on managing quality of service as we grow. Not just uptime, but overall responsiveness of the solutions. It was sage advice, and such advice and more would be described when *Site Reliability Engineering* was published in 2016, a book on how Google managed its infrastructure and solutions.

The provider sector customers continued to grow for Explorys with EPM at its core. By 2013 Explorys was getting recognized by healthcare technology analyst KLAS as a contender. Explorys had pivoted. It wasn't easy, and it took a lot

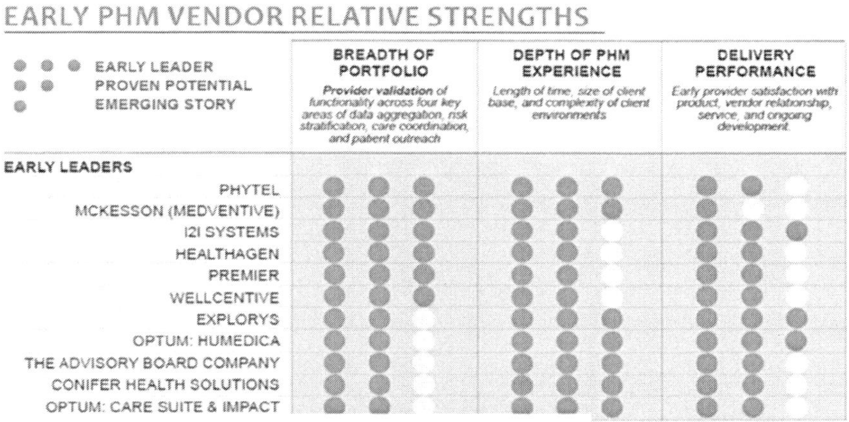

Figure 3.18 KLAS Population Health 2013. The accompanying description was: "Explorys – a leading healthcare specific BI vendor that is making particular in-roads on population health. Cloud-based with a friendly user interface that encourages physician use. Templates highlight gaps in care and physician performance. Often used on conjunction with other vendors. Lacks patient-outreach tools. Strong service and support."

of effort from the team. There were missteps a-plenty, such as a consulting company suggesting we get rid of Jira and do everything with notecards – an idea that got a bit too much consideration, but none of the missteps proved to be fatal. Now we just needed to keep up the momentum.

Embrace the Grind

But even that wasn't the whole story. That would be an oversimplification.

Data integration went through multiple iterations, going from Java ETL implementations that executed on the HDG device deployed on customer premises (this was a technical solution driven by the Data Use Agreements Explorys had at the time) to configurable extractors where the same source-to-target mapping could occur in SQL (but still issued from the HDG) to a fully functional Data Lake for data ingestion, inspection, and ETL. While new integrations adopted the latest approach available at the time, it was a testament to backward compatibility that all three of those were running at the same time across the deployments.

A more flexible approach with data integration enabled more data types to be ingested, which introduced a host of other activities. More data types and attributes mean data model additions. Data model additions mean more data standardization. More data standardization means more core pipeline changes. Additions to the data model mean changes in the analytic engines, which means additions to MDL and RDL, which means coordination with the Services team. All of this means changes to solutions like SuperMart and applications so customers can utilize the data. Never underestimate the challenges of squeezing a lot of information into a confined visual space, much less making it coherent. All of this is forward progress, but it is work. And work that needs to be coordinated.

And don't break anything.

We periodically keep revisiting how to expand and manage the infrastructure. Should we have a technical deployment per customer? "Pods" of customers? A single multi-tenant architecture? There are pros and cons with each approach, especially with the technology available at the time and hosting in our own data center. Each customer having its own stack would guarantee the best service levels for customers but would also be wasteful. A single multi-tenant architecture is the other end of the spectrum, with maximum hardware utilization at the risk of having a single basket of eggs, so to speak. "Pods" of customers still require designing multi-tenancy into the system, but now having the extra responsibility of Pod-management (i.e., which customer goes where). The fact that Explorys had the Universe for Secondary Use and that a very large percentage of the data still needed to be aggregated in the same place meant that we kept coming back to the single multi-tenant architecture.

There is a solution to having all your eggs in one basket, though: *watch that basket.*

Managing all of this required metrics. Explorys monitored its patient counts – both across all healthcare customers as well as patients in the Universe closely. But as important as patient counts are, they are incomplete. An 18-year-old in good health is not the same kind of person as a 50-year-old with a chronic condition, nor is he like a person with multiple inpatient stays and surgeries. All are humans who require appropriate clinical care, but each can represent drastically different patient data densities. Consequently, record counts of data types were also closely monitored. How long does it take to ingest and process a dataset of 100,000 patients? It depends. An important part of getting smarter is sometimes just knowing when to keep asking questions. Every day brought a new challenge.

Board Games

Everstream was founded in 1999 and was acquired by Concurrent Computer Corporation in 2005 for $15 million. Everstream went through many business model changes – first internet radio streaming, then some wandering through various consulting projects, then Video On Demand reporting – and as a result, Everstream's Board of Directors was a bit of a mismatch. Most – if not all – of the directors had been on the board since the early days and had signed up for a different company vision, and by 2005, they were wondering if Everstream was *ever* going to return anything. Concurrent represented a chance to cash out, and despite Concurrent's history of acquiring and destroying companies, what happened to Everstream after that was not their problem. The Everstream board agreed to the acquisition. McHale left six months after the acquisition. Lougheed left about a year and a half after that.

The Everstream experience represented some hard-learned lessons, and at least one of them would be heeded: don't lose control of the board.

The Explorys board was packed with insiders (McHale, Lougheed), family of insiders (McHale's brother John McHale, an entrepreneur behind companies such as NetWorth, acquired by Compaq, NetSpeed, acquired by Cisco, and TippingPoint, acquired by 3Com), and de facto business partners (Cleveland Clinic Innovations). Having control of the board allowed Explorys to set its own product direction, something that is easy to state as a goal but hard to pull off in practice. The pivot that Explorys made from Secondary Use on provider analytic solutions in 2011 was a big risk, for example, but one formed from direct experience. The easy option would have been to continue to service Secondary Use and then to quickly sell out. Regular questioning from a board of directors should be expected, but a combative board can be trouble, especially when not aligned on strategy. The pivot was a bold move that could only have been pulled off with board control.

The Explorys board would expand in 2012 during a funding round, but not to the point where the insiders or insider-allies were outnumbered.

Chapter 4

Moving a Startup

Finding a Place for People and Stuff

Moving offices was another Explorys' core competency. This sounds like an antiquated skill in the post-Covid19 era, but this was a very serious matter for the company.

First Office

The first office Explorys occupied (Fall 2009 to July 2010) was in the Triangle Apartment complex in Cleveland's University Circle, right next to Case Western Reserve University. There was an open work area, a conference room, and a little break room in the back. We managed to squeeze about a dozen people in there. It was a retail storefront that had previously been the sales office for the Uptown Redevelopment project of the area, and before that, a Time Warner Cable billing office. I know this because someone once arrived at our office and tried to return their cable settop to me.

The Triangle was (and still is) an apartment complex, and another time a resident upstairs left their water running and it overflowed to our office below. Late one Friday afternoon,

 DOI: 10.4324/9781003491590-4

we were watching a bulge form in the ceiling tiles, and it seemed to be growing in real time. We were looking at each other thinking "is that *really* happening?" We were able to get the desks out of the way just in time before it burst, and then were able to get in touch with building maintenance to get into the apartment and shut off the water. I think we had somebody interviewing and a new hire in the office at that moment as well. "Welcome to Explorys! Trust us, it's going to be awesome!" Had this happened just an hour or two later, we would have been gone and it would have been flooding all weekend. The joy of small offices.

This office was my favorite in terms of walking because, within two minutes, I could be strolling around the museums in Wade Oval. I would go out for a lunch-walk most days to clear my head and think. About a month after moving into this office, I was out for a walk when I was stopped by an old couple in a car asking me how to get to the hospital. In University Circle, "hospital" requires disambiguation, so I had to then engage them in some conversation to find out whether they were going to Cleveland Clinic, University Hospitals, or the Veterans Administration. After engaging them in some conversation and determining their intended destination, I then provided directions and some parking tips. This kept happening every six to eight weeks. I must have one of those faces.

The Triangle Apartment storefronts (and parking lot) were later converted into the Uptown district. Mitchell's Ice Cream is pretty much where the first office was.

It was a Friday afternoon in late June 2010, and we were in the process of packing up for the next office. As we had only been in our first real office since the previous Fall we didn't have that much, but we had accumulated *enough*. Enough to require some minor packing. We were supposed to be taking everything home and then showing up the following Monday at our new office, the newly built Global Cardiovascular

Figure 4.1 Explorys first office (2009). That was the whole office, plus a conference room. That is my ball-chair on the right.

Innovation Center on the Cleveland Clinic campus at E. 100th and Cedar Road, about 1.5 miles west. The agreement was that Explorys was to get 35 or so parking spots behind the building, and then overflow parking in a surface lot across the street. At the literal last minute, the Cleveland Clinic tried to change the deal to 20 spots behind the building, with overflow parking in the Muni Lot. The negotiation tactic from the Clinic was straightforward: "What's the big deal? That's where our nurses park."

The *Muni Lot* was shorthand for Cleveland's Municipal Parking Lot. It's a large windswept parking lot astride Route 2 and the railroad tracks near the Browns stadium downtown. It's a great place to tailgate, drink, and barf with 60,000 of your best friends, but if your workplace is in University Circle – where Cleveland Clinic Main Campus is – it leaves the commuter four miles distant and in need of a bus. Not exactly premium parking for that work location. You can bet your bottom dollar the Cleveland Clinic didn't make its physicians park there.

Oof. Somebody just said the quiet part out loud.

The move was paused. The Cleveland Clinic might treat their own employees that way, but not us. Explorys wasn't just a building tenant; it was supposed to be an on-paper business partner. The parking standoff fortunately didn't last long as we received the originally agreed-upon parking, and the move commenced. But it got a little tense for a day or two.

Second Office

The newly built Global Cardiovascular Innovation Center (GCIC) was Explorys' home from July 2010 to November 2012 at E. 100th and Cedar. Did I mention it was *new*? It had new building look. New building feel. New building smell. This was not a former Time Warner Cable billing office. Not that the billing office was a bad place, but being across the street from Cleveland Clinic Main Campus helped people feel *clinical.* And engaged. You could even hear it – helicopters took off and landed every day on the roof of the emergency services building a block or so away. That was a real person with real problems being transported somewhere. Lives were saved every day. And some lives weren't. Death was a part of healthcare too. This is where the action happened.

I enjoyed eating lunch at the main Clinic cafeteria. I thought the food was good, and there was always a mix of staff, visitors, and patients – a constant motivating reminder of why we were doing this. This is also back when the Clinic had already made the decision to only stock diet soda drinks and low-fat snacks in the vending machines, a small but noticeable improvement. And this was also shortly after the Clinic banned smoking for employees in 2007, which was initially an unpopular edict, but it really does make sense as smoking is a major risk factor in a number of cancers, and like it or not, the Clinic staff needed to set the example. This was also when there was a McDonalds next to the main cafeteria. This was actually on campus and *inside* the facility, and the only place where one could not only legally purchase a high-octane non-diet Coke but also a quarter pounder with cheese and supersized fry. All this at the #1 heart center in the United States. It did a brisk business as far as I could tell, even with customers wearing scrubs. I'm sure the Clinic wasn't thrilled with this unhealthy dichotomy, and the alleged backstory was that this McDonalds had a long-term lease that somehow couldn't be revoked. Eventually, the McDonalds was replaced with something less medically ironic, but it took a few years.

The Cleveland Clinic used to have a fantastic two-story library in the Lerner Research Center at the time, and with historical displays and chock full of medical texts, it was a great place to go for some quiet offsite work. The library was only a two-minute walk from the GCIC and had lots of little workspaces as well as access to the Cleveland Clinic Public wifi. Have wifi, will travel. Another great on-campus hangout space was the rooftop of the Miller building, which had an outdoor patio with a great view of downtown Cleveland and University Circle. And wifi. Always wifi. While the rooftop patio still exists today, unfortunately, the old library was turned into more offices.

The GCIC had its own benefits though. My favorite part of this office was the innovation room on the second floor that had a great work-table with monitors on each end, with bar-stool-height swivel chairs – great for collaboration. The walls were a giant whiteboard. There were two frequently utilized treadmill desks. One engineer got carried away on a project and walked seven miles in one day, which doesn't seem like that much, but try it on a treadmill – it's painful. The room was supposed to be a common area for all the tenants of the building, but we tended to hog it (*sorry*!).

The office temperature control mechanism became not just a conversation point but a rallying cry. It was a round knob with a "–" on one side and "+" on the other, with no numbers. I'm pretty sure people don't administer drugs this way. There was unconfirmed speculation that this control was an artifice just to make the tenants feel better and didn't actually do anything, and our testing went along the lines of "let's have 'More Plus' and see what happens! Yes! MORE PLUS!" That became the catchphrase for doing something bigger and better. Explorys t-shirts were made with a picture of that knob and More Plus on the back.

Explorys started with two smaller offices on the second floor that were connected by knocking down a wall. The DevOps team started in a converted wet-lab space that was turned into an office on the other side of the floor. Another office was added on the third floor. By mid-2012, people were sitting on top of each other. This was when Explorys started handing out Beats by Dr Dre headphones to employees, a

Figure 4.2 Cleveland Clinic Global Cardiovascular Innovation Center (GCIC) in 2024. That's pretty much the way it looked in 2010 when it was built and Explorys was there.

Figure 4.3 Explorys office in the GCIC in 2010/2011.

Figure 4.4 Explorys office in the GCIC in 2010/2011. If you look at the wall, you can see this was a wet-lab converted into offices.

practice which went on for years. First, Beats headphones were cool. Second, they were very practical given the employee density. I still have mine.

The building was primarily designed for wet-labs and small offices. The wet-labs were designed for one person in a back office and two people in the lab, and the building's bathroom capacity was sized for those expectations. We would pack in about ten people in the same space. Consequently, one frequently needed to hunt floor-to-floor when nature called.

Eventually we ran out of space because we couldn't keep tearing up wet-labs in the building. Time for another move.

Third Office

The third office (November 2012 to August 2016) was in the Old Cleveland Playhouse complex on Carnegie on the west edge of the Cleveland Clinic Main Campus at 8501 Carnegie. The Clinic had purchased the complex after the Cleveland Playhouse theater company moved to Playhouse Square downtown. Technically, we were in "the old Sears building" section of the complex, whose previous tenant was the Cleveland Museum of Contemporary Art. Coincidentally, that museum moved down the street near where Explorys' first office was with a new building.

The Old Playhouse complex was the craziest office location I've ever worked in. And it wasn't "we have a ping pong table and bean bag chairs" crazy, though we did have a ping pong table. The complex was old and massive. It wasn't entirely clear to most people where the back fire escape of our section actually led and how much of the team we would get back if anybody went out that way. That particular door led to a warren of rooms and staircases, and good luck finding your way in the dark and/ or urgent conditions. And that was just the upstairs area. The basement was both huge and divided up in a horror-movie-creepy, single-unshielded-lightbulb-dangling-from-the-ceiling kind of way. It was the perfect place for Cleveland-area SWAT teams to practice room-clearing drills, and there were targets with spent stun gun wires lying about. There were also pallets of Clinic medical supplies that were either inventory overflow from next door or were stockpiled for regional disaster response. You know – *normal office stuff.*

After we moved in, we received a great tour from the building supervisor, Maurice, who knew the history of the complex because his father had been the building supervisor for 40 years back when the Playhouse was in operation at that location. The Playhouse had an amazing history, as Margaret Hamilton, Joel Grey, and Paul Newman once performed there. We explored the various stages occasionally on subsequent unsanctioned tours, with the oldest theater from the 1920s being my favorite.

There was also a barbeque place called Hot Sauce Williams a block or so away, which had an autographed picture of actor/comedian Robin Williams on the wall made out to the restaurant. I imagine this would have horrified Robin's cardiologist if he found out that Robin had flown a few thousand miles to Cleveland for heart surgery and then apparently went for some post-op recovery spicy ribs.

Figure 4.5 Explorys engineers at the Old Cleveland Playhouse during a major upgrade.

Figure 4.6 **Author standing in front of the Old Cleveland Playhouse (2016).**

Figure 4.7 **Cleveland Fire Department responding to a fire alarm for Explorys at the Old Cleveland Playhouse. This happened a few times.**

Figure 4.8 The front lobby of the Explorys office in the Old Cleveland Playhouse (2013). The upper level and curved stairs had been put in place by the prior tenant, the Cleveland Museum of Modern Art. Permission from Jen Hearn.

Figure 4.9 The center work area in the Explorys office in the Old Cleveland Playhouse (2013). This has a "former department store" feel because it was a Sears many decades ago. Permission from Jen Hearn.

But going out for food was just one option because the Playhouse was the office where Explorys lunches really became a thing. Lunch was provided a couple of times a week from area restaurants – Tommy's from the nearby Coventry neighborhood in Cleveland Heights, known for its hippy-and-Mediterranean fare, was always a favorite, but there was a healthy mix. Sometimes pizza and pasta, sometimes Indian, sometimes sandwiches. I'm not doing enough justice to the front-desk folks who coordinated all of this. There was a ritual to it as well: food carts would be wheeled all the way from the front door to the kitchen area in the back, guaranteeing that everyone could both see *and smell* what was coming. Then the door to the kitchen would be shut with an agonizing 10 to 15 minutes of setup. It was bad form to hover, so people would continue working with one eye on the door. Then it would burst open and initiate a mad scramble to line up. No words were necessary. Lunch days could also find members of the Cleveland Clinic Police who just happened to be on patrol in our office at the noon hour, just to make sure things were safe and secure in this section of main campus. They were always welcome.

By early 2016, people were, again, practically sitting on top of each other. The cavernous main room was absolutely jammed, and there was a desk everywhere it was possible to put one, even in a round "Sun Room" in the back next to the kitchen originally meant as a hangout area but was turned into dedicated workspace. The Services team had moved around the corner into a former theater performance warm-up space, and that was packed to the gills as well. It was time for another move.

Fourth Office

The fourth office (August 2016 to Summer 2018) was at 1111 Superior, downtown Cleveland. We were on the 26th to 28th floors – the former Eaton Corporation executive floors, refurbished for the proletariat, with an outstanding view of downtown and Lake Erie. The St. Patrick's Day parade went right in front of the building. While downtown lacked the clinical atmosphere of University Circle, it made it extremely easy for out-of-town travelers because of multiple hotels and food options within walking distance from the office. As a food-aside, Explorys lunches silently disappeared the moment we moved into 1111 Superior. That said, one just needed to get to the office and everything else was easy. The downtown Heinen's grocery store was a favorite of mine as it was set in the old Cleveland Trust Rotunda, was architecturally gorgeous, had a great salad bar, and was a five-minute walk. The wine machines on the second floor also made for a nice after-work meeting place. The Rotunda – pre-Heinens – was featured in multiple movies: *The Avengers* (2012, as a bank being attacked by the Chitauri) and *Captain America: Winter Soldier* (2014, as a Hydra secret lair), which both had significant segments filmed in Cleveland.

Figure 4.10 1111 Superior in 2024. Explorys had the top three floors in 2016–2018.

Figure 4.11 One of our software engineers was tragically turned into Poppy the Balloon Snowman. This picture, however, does show the nice view that Poppy inherited with Lake Erie in the background.

Figure 4.12 The spiral staircase in 1111 Superior turned into an RNA helix. The Explorys office was in what was formerly Eaton Corporation's executive floors, remodeled for the proletariat.

During our time in this office, I was stopped twice by drivers while I was walking in from a nearby parking garage who asked me where the Justice Center was and how to get there. Different destination, but people still needed driving directions. I must still have had one of those faces.

Chapter 5

Acquisition Due Diligence

Getting Shopped

The First Suitor

The first acquisition due diligence process started in November 2014, and it wasn't with IBM. To say it was a distraction was an understatement. Virtual Clean Rooms were established to provide documentation on all parts of the business. From a technical standpoint, it required providing our codebase to a third party and documenting any and all libraries or external software components we were using and whether we were in compliance. We had collectively been attentive to these points over the years, preferring software licenses such as Apache, MIT, or Mozilla for components, but it's still a lot of effort when you need to *prove it*.

There was a standard pitch about the Explorys technical architecture that was part of sales presentations. The technical architecture served a supporting role to our clinical functionality, and this was a good thing. But now we needed

DOI: 10.4324/9781003491590-5

presentation-worthy documentation on everything – even the internal parts.

I did a technical overview for half a day at the InterContinental Hotel at the Cleveland Clinic. I think from an engineering standpoint we looked "ok," but I'm also sure our preparations looked a bit rough. Properly preparing for acquisition due diligence is a lot of work.

I'm not sure why this didn't proceed further, but by December 2014, it seemed like there wasn't any further momentum on this path.

Most critically during this phase of Explorys, the financials were locked up, and we couldn't expand the clusters. That was a problem for a company that was still on the rise.

The Second Suitor

But Explorys wasn't lonely for long. In early 2015, there was another suitor, and we were engaged with this one for what felt like almost two months before it fell through.

From an engineering standpoint, we leveraged everything that was prepared from the first due diligence and then added to it. I think we looked pretty respectable.

Our financials were unfortunately still locked up, and we still couldn't expand the clusters. This was becoming a serious problem.

The Third Suitor

Practically the week after the second suitor's efforts ended, IBM swooped in. IBM had been showing up every six months in the years prior to acquisition and discreetly kicking the tires.

There was a week-long due diligence process with multiple meeting rooms at the InterContinental Hotel at the Cleveland Clinic. I called my wife on a break on Monday morning to give her an update.

"Are they kicking the tires again?" she asked.

"No, this is an invasion" I said.

It felt like there were two dozen IBM representatives in the main conference room for the kickoff. They really seemed to be serious this time.

The central activity was filling out a ~2,000-question spreadsheet about all aspects of Explorys. HR, finance, legal, sales, and, of course, plenty of engineering questions. It was IBM's standard due diligence approach and quite thorough.

We took everything from the second due diligence effort and again added to it. Now, our third time through engineering due diligence, I think we looked pretty solid, all things considered for a startup. Source code for all the products? No problem! Added to the clean room. Documentation on all the third party libraries? No problem! It's even been reviewed by legal. Cluster specifications? Cluster utilization and ingested data statistics? Software architecture documentation? Product documentation? No problem! No problem! No problem! No problem!

There is always room for improvement, and I'm not suggesting that we had perfectly documented everything, but we would not have been that prepared had IBM been the *first* suitor. That's for certain.

And right then, at our most excellent moment together in due diligence, an IDC vendor evaluation came out in April 2015 where Explorys was named a leader. Upper-right-hand corner, folks. Not bad for a software startup from Cleveland.

I had a long exposure to IBM from back at my time at Key Bank. I spoke at a CICS User Conference in the late 1990s. Many people know about IBM Corporate Songbooks of days past, but that also extended to specific products – and I have an CICS Songbook autographed by Ben Riggins, one of the lead designers of CICS. I had also used MQ Series, the messaging product, and Db2, and even knew my way around several mainframe utilities. I devoured IBM Redbooks by the yard.

Figure 5.1 IDC MarketScape: US Healthcare Provider Clinical and Financial Analytics Standalone Platform 2015 Vendor Assessment, doc # HI255139, April 2015. The IDC MarketScape vendor analysis model is designed to provide an overview of the competitive fitness of technology and suppliers in a given market. The research methodology utilizes a rigorous scoring methodology based on both qualitative and quantitative criteria that results in a single graphical illustration of each supplier's position within a given market. The Capabilities score measures supplier product, go-to-market, and business execution in the short term. The Strategy score measures alignment of supplier strategies with customer requirements in a 3–5-year timeframe. Supplier market share is represented by the size of the icons.

I admired IBM's early support of Java and IBM's support for Java APIs for its products. Though I didn't see IBM much in the Hadoop or big data ecosystem at that time, I was nonetheless excited. IBM was a big tech company with a storied history.

IBM was going to accelerate Explorys and push us even further to the upper-right. Fetch your fucking umbrellas, because it's going to rain servers and customers around here!

At least that is what we thought.

Chapter 6

IBM Watson Health: Formation

Formation and Timeline

IBM had been in healthcare for a long time before Watson Health. IBM Research had been undertaking various healthcare projects, and the consulting arm/s of IBM had been performing a variety of custom healthcare projects (typically on-prem deployments) utilizing IBM products such as Db2 (database), UDMH (healthcare data model), MDM (identity management and entity resolution), MQ Series (messaging), and IIB (integration bus), among others. The development of Watson for Oncology pre-dated the creation of the Watson Health division by several years. IBM had also once been in medical devices long ago with a division in Minnesota, I was told.

But in general IBM didn't have much in the way of healthcare *applications*. IBM would sell you a set of tires, an engine, and a steering wheel, and the consulting hours to put them together, but it couldn't sell you a *vehicle*. That's what Watson Health was going to address. This was a reasonable and admirable ambition.

 DOI: 10.4324/9781003491590-6

Moonshot

IBM CEO Ginni Rometty made bold statements about IBM and healthcare at the formation of the Watson Health division in April 2015:

> If you go back in time, we have participated in some of the most glorious moments of history, whether it might have been the first systems that ever did census and landing a man on the moon," said Ginni Rometty, chairman and CEO of IBM, on PBS's Charlie Rose talk show. "I'm telling you our moonshot will be the impact we will have on healthcare. It has already started. We will do our part to change the face of healthcare. I am absolutely positive about it.

And this also wasn't the only moonshot as the United States had also declared a moonshot initiative for cancer treatment in January 2016, which IBM praised. I don't blame IBM for supporting this initiative, as nobody likes cancer. The cancer moonshot was aimed primarily around IBM's Watson for Oncology efforts, which pre-dated the IBM Watson Health division and were an outgrowth of the IBM Jeopardy effort from IBM Research.

Watson Health Cloud

Anyone familiar with acquisitions knows that successfully integrating a *single* company is hard. What IBM tried with Watson Health was well beyond that. On top of creating the entirely new Watson Health division in April 2015, IBM acquired a bunch of healthcare software companies –

- Curam (social services software, acquired 2011. Moved into Watson Health after the formation of the division in April 2015)

- Explorys (healthcare and life sciences population analytics, acquired April 2015)
- Phytel (healthcare analytics and patient contact, acquired April 2015)
- Merge Healthcare (imaging, Fall 2015)
- Truven (claims analytics, April 2016)

– to seed this new division and then also mix in several IBM Research healthcare assets. At the formation, most of the actual products and most of the actual customers at the formation of the division were from *acquisitions*. The overall Watson Health strategy, though, was to rebuild everything that had just been acquired in the "Watson Health Cloud" on SoftLayer.

It shouldn't take a software or management guru to see the potential downsides of this approach. For starters, there *were* some overlaps in acquisition functionality, which were obviously not the fault of any individual acquisition, but even that wasn't the biggest problem. The strategic rebuild plan, while probably beautiful when viewed from 250,000 feet, placed scant priority on evolving the acquisitions and their already deployed solutions to keep their existing customer bases happy (and growing). This effectively would require hitting a multi-year pause for the existing solutions, and most customers don't appreciate that. In too many ways, Watson Health operated like a billion-dollar research project that was disconnected from the market yet still burdened with the financial expectations of a public company that wanted quarter-by-quarter stratospheric results. I think even the IBM top brass would have to grudgingly admit in retrospect that this was crazy-making.

Mergers and Acquisitions: The On-Paper Idea vs. Reality

Mergers and acquisitions (M&A) have been a staple of businesses ever since the first corporations were created. They always look promising on paper and invariably turn out to be more challenging and more work than anyone thought possible. But people keep coming back to the M&A path because it seems like a shortcut to growth and success. The tech sector is no stranger to this, including some things that we take for granted. Google acquired YouTube in 2006. Microsoft added PowerPoint via acquiring Forethought in 1987 and Visio in 2000. Apple acquired FingerWorks in 2005 for key components in the first iPhone. It can work.

I saw M&A up close several times in my own career. When I started as a systems analyst at a regional financial institution called Society Bank in the early 1990s, I lived through a merger between two financial institutions in Cleveland that were right down the street from each other, Society Bank and AmeriTrust. The collapsing and consolidating of org charts and departments didn't affect me much at the time because I was early in my career, but I could quickly see that this wasn't pain-free on any level. Jobs were changed. Data centers were closed. Systems needed to be converted.

A request for volunteers was put out for one of the system conversions so I came in for a 4 am shift. I was there to answer phones and to fetch people just in case. The conversion schedule was practically down to the minute. The system operators would cut a backup tape and then a bike messenger would race down the street between data centers with a big plastic reel strapped to his back in a delivery bag. Then the bike messenger would race back the street for another tape. And on it went. Believe it or not, that was the fastest way at the time for large scale data transfers between institutions. Whatever I saw that morning was at best only 0.1% of what was happening overall, but it was a lesson in how much effort it took to plan and execute a successful systems migration.

To an MBA or strategist a merger is simple, like A + B = C. Good + Good = Awesome; it says so on the graph. As profits must ever be increased, the equation becomes A + B – C = D after redundancies and inefficiencies are removed, which increases awesomeness. But the on-the-ground-reality is that mergers are more like two planets crashing into each other. The "redundancies" more often than not turn out to be *people* and the "inefficiencies" frequently turn out to be *their jobs*. It is also not always clear that the two objects really belong together, and whether things get bigger and better only becomes evident after the shaking stops and the atmosphere heals.

I lived through another bank merger a few years later when Society Bank merged with Key Bank. Another org-chart collision. More migrations. Now the headquarters were moving between cities as Key was formerly headquartered in Albany, NY. This might be a part of life, but it's not easy. Both of those mergers however were generally successful. But not pain free.

I lived through yet another version as a startup when Everstream was acquired by Concurrent Computer Corporation, and this was much more *in-your-face* as Everstream was about a 25-person company. Concurrent seemed to have a habit of acquiring companies and somehow turning them to dust. There was a video streaming company in England I was told had 100 people when they were acquired and had about a dozen by the time Everstream was acquired. There was another Philadelphia-based video streaming acquisition that I visited once before it was shut down. Everstream went through a similar trajectory over the years. On one hand it's reassuring to know that the corporate destruction isn't personal, but it's hard *not* to feel that way when you are going through it.

But the experience I had most on my mind was from the mid-to-late 1990s, from one of Key's vendors that I worked with closely. Key utilized an early Java Application Server platform called NetDynamics for web application development, back when the internet as we all know it today was emerging: the web browser, and protocols like HTML and HTTP were all created during that timeframe and evolving fast. The Java programming language was also created in this period. Companies wanted scalable and interactive "web solutions" but those weren't easy to put together, and that was what Application Servers helped with, and NetDynamics had an innovative product in that space. Sun Microsystems, the creators of Java and a leader in high-end computer workstations, acquired NetDynamics in 1998. It seemed like a great fit.

Then the fun started.

Netscape acquired one of NetDynamics' competitors called Kiva. America Online (AOL), which was huge at the time, set up a partnership with Netscape. Then Sun and Netscape/AOL established "iPlanet" – a combined product brand, where NetDynamics and Kiva crashed into each other. This wound up effectively killing them both, which was unfortunate because they were among the top Application Servers in the market, if not the top two.

That type of "merging" can create intense market confusion. If a customer has spent years building solutions on product X, determining whether X will continue to be supported is a huge concern. It wasn't clear which application server would be the winner, making life within iPlanet chaotic and unpleasant with bitter turf wars. Even merging "the best parts of each" can still create a situation for customers where there still isn't a clean upgrade path. Customers eventually decided that picking an *entirely different vendor* would be a safer solution than continuing to bet on iPlanet.

iPlanet wasn't the first and won't be the last organization to walk that path. It is a lesson that IBM Watson Health would learn the hard way.

Bluewashing – Summer 2015

The half-year of acquisition due diligence was finally over and we were a part of IBM now, and becoming a part of IBM requires *Bluewashing*. This is a real term, and refers to all aspects of IBM onboarding, such as re-registering employee benefits, re-banding employee job titles, changing payroll systems, moving email (we must have been the last people on the planet to *start* using Lotus Notes in 2015), learning new travel and expense processes, new budgeting and ordering systems, re-issuing IBM standard-image laptops, and so forth. These tasks are a lot of work, but they do make sense in being able to manage and execute within a single organization with consistency. IBM assigns an Integration Executive to each acquisition to help manage and coordinate these processes and many others, and the executive assigned to Explorys was very good. Managing the integration of an acquisition required a lot of thankless and behind-the-scenes work.

We were excited to get going.

Instead, we waited.

One of the initial sticking points was Job Banding. Job Banding is a big deal at IBM. Job Bands range from one to ten, with professional bands being six to ten. Executive bands start at D and to go A. We had to wait *months* for the Job Bands to get worked out for the staff, including me. The delays didn't inspire confidence, and the explanation was that "Job Banding is complex" which I'm sure was true, but we weren't the first software company that IBM had acquired. It felt like new math to IBM, which was odd. Eventually our Integration Executive was able to unclog this backup. I'm not sure what the cause was, but it probably stunk.

We got some strange vibes when going through IBM HR onboarding when the HR representatives asked "what are things that Watson could do for businesses?" People were supposed to write down ideas and then talk about them as group. This was at an IBM employee onboarding meeting, where most people's expectations were that required employee paperwork would be distributed and filled out, obtaining their respective IBM Serial Numbers (which sounds like something that would be stuck on the underside of an aforementioned standard-issue laptop, but for employees), and then get back to work. The discussion topic was a little odd but not terrible, but the bigger issue was that it wasn't clear what Watson really was. Nobody at Explorys was trying to be difficult, but when speaking to a technical crowd the details matter. The HR onboarding lead responded with "Watson is AI ... like NLP (Natural Language Processing)." A proper technical overview of Watson would have been useful in this moment, but that wasn't what was happening. This was Jeopardy on the brain. This messaging was not the fault of our Integration Executive, this was a Watson marketing messaging set from the CEO.

Welcome to IBM.

We still couldn't add servers to our clusters, which was also a concern. We were still waiting on that as well, and although our Integration Executive advocated for us those decisions were being managed by higher-ups at Watson Health for the time being and things were on hold. Somebody mentioned that we should look at SoftLayer, a hosting company that IBM acquired from 2013. One of our DevOps engineers did and I remember talking to him after he had gone through the SoftLayer hosting calculator. "This shit is really expensive," he said. He had a concerned and confused look on his face. "I'm pretty sure I entered the specs correctly, but these costs can't be right."

It turns out those *were* the actual numbers, but we will return to that later.

Deep Bluewashing – Summer 2015

There is a deeper level of Bluewashing though, with the intention to swap out everything that is *not IBM* to its IBM equivalent. True Blue, so to speak. There is benefit to IBM, for sure, in having all of IBM's products powered by all of IBM's other products. There were a few challenges though. First, Explorys

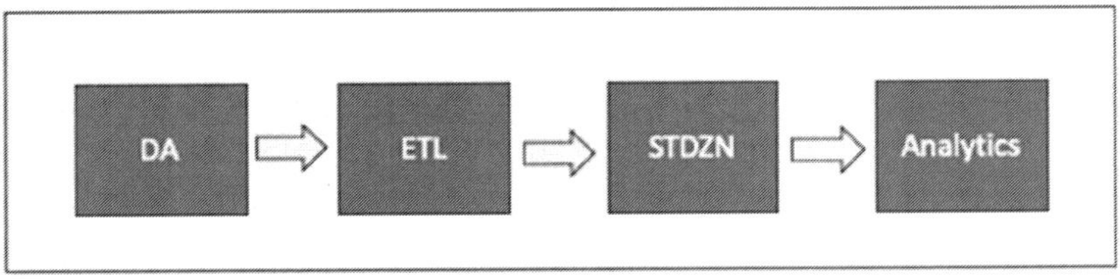

Figure 6.1 Overly simplified customer onboarding process.

was starting from a position of using no IBM products. Second, given IBM's large catalog of product offerings this was an enormous undertaking, and it wasn't always clear what the "right" answer was, even if we wanted to swap something out.

One of the first IBM products to descend on Explorys was DataStage. The context was for customer data onboarding and it was IBM's data transformation tool, or at least one of them. It was Summer of 2015 and this coincided with ongoing analysis and concern of how to optimize the Explorys customer onboarding process which at the time was understood to look like this –

– where:

- **DA** = Data Acquisition to integrate with source systems and extract required data, preferably in original form (or "raw")
- **ETL** = Extract, Transform Load source data to the Explorys internal common model
- **STDZN** = Standardize many dozens of attributes with "local" values to standard codesets, taxonomies, and ontologies
- **Analytics** = Generate clinical measures and registries, some of them out-of-the-box offerings, and some custom per customer

The picture looks simple enough – bring in data, transform it, standardize it, and then analyze it. The problem was that issues had a habit of getting caught in the Analytics validation phase and frequently got ping-ponged back to the earlier steps in the process, and the ponging and pinging were amplified as the size of the implementation grew. The process *generally worked*, but it wasn't entirely clear where the most expensive parts of the process were, and just as importantly, *why* and what could be done about it.

The people representing DataStage were very confident in their opinion that *not* using DataStage was the reason why we had process inefficiencies, and our problems would disappear once we started using it.

There was an immediate emphasis on DataStage's visual/graphical ETL capabilities. This was the only way to do it, we were told. Admittedly, visual-line-drawing-between-boxes tooling looks great for demos and can also be very useful for prototypes. But this type of tooling tends to work well for when data is simple, and then it hits a wall when things get complex. Then people go back to coding. Given that health-care data is anything but simple, the Explorys METL team was *already* at the point of being comfortable with coding. Engineering prepared a 30+ page document of real-life ETL examples in an attempt to explain what was really happening.

It also became clear that DataStage seemed to be firmly positioned against the Hadoop stack, which was odd, not only for the times but also because IBM had its own Hadoop distribution. We're getting a bit ahead of ourselves on that point. We were given access to a large presentation where DataStage argued against the overall effectiveness of Hadoop. This was the official IBM stance, at least as far as this product was concerned, and it felt like an echo of the IBM guy on stage at Hadoop World 2009 talking about spreadsheets. There were a few slides from this 2013 deck worth pointing out, such as one titled "Why can InfoSphere Information Server run Data Integration Processes 10x-15x faster than Hadoop MapReduce?":

[Slide notes]

We are going to drill into this issue of MapReduce performance versus DataStage performance for Big Data Integration. This issue is critical to IBM's big customers.

Our leading data warehouse, Hadoop distribution, and data integration competitors all describe Hadoop MapReduce as a massively scalable distributed storage and processing system that is idea for running large data integration workloads.

The narrative is not quite accurate. Hadoop MapReduce supports application scale-out through distributed processing of large data sets across clusters of computers. However, Hadoop does not support efficient, high performance processing of large data sets across many nodes.

To understand why, let's look at the original design goals for Hadoop MapReduce.

Hadoop MapReduce was designed originally to provide fine-grained fault tolerance at the task level. Each Map writes intermediate results to disk. Each Reduce pulls data from disk. This design for fault tolerance comes at the expense of significantly lower performance.

DataStage was designed for high-performance, not fault tolerance. DataStage streams data between operators without writing intermediate results to disk. DataStage's pipelining and partitioning parallelism works within a node and across many nodes.

DataStage runs data integration processes 10x-15x than Hadoop MapReduce because DataStage was designed for high performance while MapReduce was designed for fault tolerance

Nearly the entire Explorys data infrastructure was built on Hadoop, and our real-life experience showed that it actually worked pretty well for what it did. But DataStage proponents (at least the ones we were talking to) were trying to tell us that it didn't work *at all*. We were completely talking past each other. To make matters worse, the DataStage presentation made some misleading comparisons and outdated interpretations.

First, DataStage was arguing that MapReduce was not an efficient engine for low-latency query engines, which was old news. Everybody knew that in 2009 when trying out Apache Hive, a SQL query engine built on the MapReduce framework. But people who still made those claims years later missed the point about what Apache Hive *could* do, such as being able to query terabytes of data over a large cluster using SQL. That alone was a non-trivial feat, especially at the time, because even if a query ran in minutes, the alternative tended to be *not running at all*. Besides, we had already been using Cloudera's Impala query engine, which was implemented in C++ and ran in persistent concurrent processes, on the Explorys Data Lake successfully for internal usage. Impala was another advancement in the Hadoop ecosystem and spawned multiple query-engine clones such as Presto, Drill, and SparkSQL, and Impala itself was inspired by the Google Dremel paper. Dremel described a distributed interactive query system over columnar storage that could query trillion-row tables in seconds.

Second, DataStage would continue to argue that we should avoid MapReduce, but then would point us to an article about Apache Spark. Apache Spark was a framework we were already familiar with (I had someone present on Spark in the Cleveland Big Data Meetup in 2012) and Spark was positioned as a next generation distributing processing framework, learning from MapReduce and extending the capabilities, particularly for iterative algorithms such as graph processing. But Spark was still designed to operate and integrate with Hadoop environments, a point that DataStage either missed or ignored. And stranger still, DataStage seemed be arguing against using Spark as well. DataStage's summary position was effectively "don't use open source."

And the differences didn't stop there. DataStage, on top of not supporting Hadoop, also required running as a native Windows application. Nearly everybody at Explorys was running on Macs.

Explorys had built its own Domain Specific Language (DSL) for ETL work that ran in our Data Lake cluster, which could then publish transform data to our Data Reservoir cluster for downstream processing. This DSL was also backward compatible to the previous ETL models that Explorys had created, all of which had instances still running, particularly for older customers. The ETLs could be executed via a web interface, and we had some data inspection tools built in. It took a significant amount of engineering to pull this off, and we had a sizable team already using it in production.

I'm sure that DataStage is a reasonable product, and that there are people successfully using DataStage somewhere in the world. But there were multiple reasons why DataStage wasn't a great fit *for Explorys*. At some point moving to a commercially available ETL tool was probably a good idea, but we needed to move to a tool that supported the best aspects of how we currently worked and didn't represent a backstep in functionality.

This probably was the beginning of our reputation of "Those Explorys people. They think they know best." If we had attitudes, it was because we had competed successfully in the healthcare marketplace and we sought the best approach for solutions, whether or not the ideas came from IBM.

Home-Made Problems – 2015–2017

Explorys came to IBM with its own issues, and one of them was its sales function. At the time of IBM acquisition, the sales VP had been on board less than 100 days, and over half the sales force had been let go and the team was in rebuild mode. In fairness to all the salespeople that ever worked at Explorys, the job of a salesperson is hard enough but made even harder when needing to coordinate with Explorys' leadership team for clear and consistent directions and messaging.

A related issue was Explorys' Go To Market approach. When people think about *raising revenue,* most people typically think about *sales.* But there is another aspect to raising revenue and that is the ability to *recognize revenue* from an accounting standpoint. After being *sold,* things must be *delivered* to the terms of the Statement of Work. Coincidentally, there was another due diligence concern regarding financial controls given that it was run through a single person, a situation probably not unique to startups but still worthy of note.

Explorys contracts and associated Statements of Work tended to be a bit loose. Take for example, a statement for three clinical registries and ten clinical measures for Explorys' Enterprise Performance Manager (EPM) product. From a delivery standpoint the registries and measures could be delivered iteratively and that is a good thing as customers could see value sooner than later. Unfortunately, from an accounting standpoint that's not the way it works. Statements of Work are all-or-nothing. And apparently Explorys had a bunch of contracts that were in the order of ten registries and 50 clinical measures each described as "to be defined later."

This made the financial folks at IBM pull their hair out, and I don't blame them for being frustrated. Explorys would have eventually been bitten by this at some point, it just happened to be IBM that provided the reality check. Given IBM's expectations of Watson Health having immediate hockey-stick revenue growth, this was like throwing gasoline on the problem. But it doesn't excuse the way that Explorys had been contracting.

When it was getting off the ground, Explorys was just happy to get a customer to sign *any* Statement of Work, and Explorys isn't unique in this regard. It's easy to say *Sure, We'll Do That! Sounds Good!* just to get a deal closed. But in Explorys' defense, it had made great strides in putting together a large portfolio of productized out-of-the-box analytics with EPM. But contracting and constructing actionable and manageable Statements of Work is an art. It must overlap with product and service capabilities yet is a distinct activity and skill and the devil is in the details as the saying goes. It needs to account for all manner of customer configuration needs and edge cases. It's not easy. All bills eventually come due, and defining smaller and more specific deliverables is clearly a lesson learned.

Bluewashing – Fall 2015

We moved into the Fall of 2015 still without a sense of who was driving product management or how any of this was going to work. Explorys and Phytel were both acquired in April 2015 at the Watson Health division creation and both product lines were still in a holding pattern.

Enter Watson Health Cloud. Something that we had been hearing about but now was becoming a topic of discussion. We had an offsite with some of the Phytel technical team and some of the Watson Health Architecture team in September 2015 in Dallas to talk about the Explorys and Phytel product set and their respective product architectures. The Watson Health Architecture team talked about the future plans for the Watson Health Cloud.

The product overviews were a good idea to inform the other teams about important product functionality and customers, so this was a start. But hearing about the Watson Health Cloud plans was a bit un-nerving. Explorys and Phytel had customers. Watson Health Cloud was being *built*.

And it was being built on SoftLayer.

IBM's cloud situation was – pun intended – somewhat cloudy in 2015 as there were multiple hosting groups within IBM. SoftLayer was the primary consumer-facing cloud service at the time, was itself an IBM acquisition in June 2013 – less than two years before the formation of Watson Health. SoftLayer was "sort of IBM and sort of not IBM" in the sense that IBM Watson Health was paying the same price the public was paying. This started to explain what our DevOps engineer found when he was looking at the SoftLayer cost calculator earlier in the Summer.

To make it worse, from a technical perspective SoftLayer *was* a "cloud" (so that part was true) but it wasn't the same class of "cloud-native" offering as AWS, Azure, and GCP for supporting programmable infrastructure-as-a-service, at least at the time. It's primary use-cases were the static provisioning of servers

Figure 6.2 IBM Somers, NY 2015–2016. See the pyramid? IBM Somers was designed by I.M. Pei back in the 1980s. It is now closed.

for database, application, and web workloads. We got the gist that the typical customer probably had ten or fewer servers per deployment. Our footprint was well over 100 times that. Explorys managed its own infrastructure and utilized high-performance networking equipment from Arista Networks, for example, and pushed significant network traffic every day with our workloads. When we described this to IBM and SoftLayer they responded as if we were either making our utilization numbers up or had three heads and were from another planet. Neither was true, and we had the logs to prove it.

Then we had a few Watson Health Cloud offsites in IBM Somers.

Somers, New York, was a campus of IBM's past, designed in the 1980s by famed architect I.M. Pei. By the time we got there, it had a corporate post-apocalyptic feel, long before Covid-19. There was a giant parking lot with few cars. There were signs on the wall for marketing campaigns that were years out of date. There were multiple multi-story sections for workspaces connected to a shared common section for larger meeting rooms and the main cafeteria, and you could have safely fired a cannon down one of those connecting corridors at regular intervals and not hit anybody. I like old buildings, so the campus had a certain appeal, but it also presented a strange vibe for meetings to lay the foundation of the new Watson Health division. Is this our future?

This is also roughly when we started hearing about IBM's IIB and MQ Series products. The Watson Health Architecture team was having an allergic reaction to our use of Apache Kafka, a distributed messaging platform. Add another technical framework to the annoyance list.

Watson Health Cloud and SoftLayer were the future, and the general idea was that the entire Watson Health product portfolio was going to be migrated and rebuilt there. Which was ambitious to be sure. But on what timeline, exactly? On whose budgets? And what about our current customers?

Don't worry about it, I was told.

This is also when we started hearing other statements such as "give us your data" and "give us your code," after all, "you're at IBM now." We had been acquired. Bought. Purchased. Which was true as far as it went, but the intention was more like "the grown-ups will take it from here, kid!"

There were some serious issues with respect to "give us your data" requests, such as SoftLayer's HIPAA Data Use Agreement (DUA) not being compatible with a number of Explorys' customers. In a nutshell, SoftLayer had a one-size-fits-all approach, whereas Explorys accepted the union of responsibility from the DUAs it signed with its customers. Explorys was hyper-aware of security and HIPAA because one slip-up would have meant the death of the company. It was disconcerting to have these topics not taken as seriously as we took them. The issues were addressable, but they couldn't just be ignored.

There is an old-time IBM phrase about "Wild Ducks," which was apparently a favorite of TJ Watson Jr himself and about the utility of unconventional thinkers. *Treasure Wild Ducks* went the saying. What we were experiencing was that Wild Ducks sounded great on a motivational poster, but in real life, the more likely reaction within IBM was to bring out a 12-gauge to stop the quacking.

Enter our new VP of Development for Explorys, a transfer from another IBM division. While he didn't have any healthcare experience, he had big data experience – which was huge for Explorys. And as an IBM veteran with years of experience, he knew the good, bad, and ugly about how to get things done, or at least try to, at IBM. This was fortuitous.

So, in a very IBM way, he managed to put a stop to the "give us your data" and "give us your code" requests. Explorys was going to work with Watson Health Cloud as that is the strategic direction, but Watson Health Cloud also needed to work with Explorys to support the business and move it forward, he explained.

The Art of Sometimes Traveling

I started traveling a lot during this period to a number of IBM sites. Fortunately, IBM had started processes to update its travel booking and expense system and, to its credit, these processes worked well. One aspect that I really liked was per diems for food. There was a per-day allowance that was calibrated by city, so there was no need to keep all of the receipts for Starbucks and McDonalds, as well as no need to enter those receipts into an expense system, and no need for a manager to review and approve all of those mission-critical coffee and sandwich receipts.

If you spent more than the per-diem, then you owed the difference, and if you were under the per-diem, you kept it, both of which were settled electronically. It allowed employees (and approving managers) to focus on the big stuff, which was basically planes, cabs, and hotels. And those charges could be put on an American Express credit card issued to each employee. Kudos to IBM for this.

Business travel is never easy, but that's about as easy as it is ever going to get.

I flew enough to start accruing travel stories, simply by random chance. One time I was doing an out-and-back to the IBM Research Center in Yorktown Heights, NY. Out-and-backs in one day make for a long day, but they also make for easy packing because I just had my laptop backpack. I took a 6 am flight from Cleveland Hopkins Airport to LaGuardia. I don't mind flying, but I hate being late for flights. One thing I learned was just how early a 6 am flight really is. I got there before the TSA Security Checkpoints were open. And even when the security checkpoint was opened nothing else was. But at least I didn't miss the flight. Once at LaGuardia a car-service took me 40 miles north. I had meetings all day, and then I started reversing the path.

The fun started at LaGuardia. It was supposed to be a 7 pm-ish return flight and then it kept getting delayed in agonizing increments. When we finally boarded the 50-seat Regional Jet back I was sitting in my seat, dead tired, when I heard my name called. It was being called with another name I didn't recognize.

"You two are being pulled from the flight because it's overweight."

"Excuse me?" I am reasonably fast with quips but I didn't have the energy for "are you calling me overweight?" banter. Plus, I could see a bunch of empty seats. I was confused.

"You were the last two that checked in."

It might have been 50-seat Regional Jet but it was apparently still flying under Summer weight rules, which meant only 35 seats could be filled.

I started to experience the John Mulaney "Delta Airlines" routine except through American Eagle because – just like the

Figure 6.3 Author at IBM Learning Center, Armonk, NY – May 2015, a month after acquisition.

Figure 6.4 Author at IBM Ireland (2016).

Figure 6.5 Author at IBM Almaden Research Center (2016).

Figure 6.6 Author in IBM Cleveland office (2016–2017).

Figure 6.7 Author at Truven Analytics (Michigan), probably 2017.

Figure 6.8 Author at Phytel (Texas), 2016.

Figure 6.9 Author at another IBM office. I don't remember where.

Figure 6.10 Author at IBM T.J. Watson Research Center (2018). IBM's motto was "Think." It needed more of that.

standup bit – I tried to get on a plane that was delayed, then told I couldn't fly, and then was handed a meal voucher that nobody seemed to want at the airport. My new travel companion and I were then directed to a nearby Holiday Inn Express or something and we wound up walking down the street to a nearby gas station to get a late-night beer. It seemed an appropriate way to end a day of glamorous corporate travel.

The next morning I took the first flight out of LaGuardia back to Cleveland and went to the office wearing the same clothes I had on the day before.

Whatever it took to push Explorys and IBM forward.

The Passion of ZDoggMD – Fall 2015

The song "EHR State of Mind" by doctor/artist ZDoggMD came out in the Fall of 2015 and was a parody of the better-known "Empire State of Mind" by Jay-Z and Alicia Keys. It was very popular in the office and skewered the usability of EHRs along with the vendors that built them:

"bought the new software, and though we use it here, I can't use it over there, different systems everywhere"

"switched me to that EMR, 'Meaningless Abuse'"

"crappy software some vendor made us, there's nothing you can do"

"they built you a turd, doc"

"if somebody is saying it's epic, we sayin' it's epic fail"

"just a glorified billing platform, with some patient stuff tacked on"

"best practice popups will tire you, complain and they'll fire you"

"we need a new chart"

With phrases like "Meaningless Abuse" – referring to the Centers for Medicare and Medicaid Services "Meaningful Use" EHR Incentives program – and "ICD10's a disaster, meet your new robot master" this was certainly niche humor. But it was good work just the same, and even came with a well-produced video. For full disclosure, there was a quick mention of Athena Health at the end, so this was technically an advertisement, which may explain how ZDogg could afford the helicopter shot. That said, the song being an advertisement didn't invalidate the widespread EHR frustrations felt in the health-care community. Whatever was happening in IBM at the time, the song represented what Explorys also saw. There was more than an opportunity; there was a need. We weren't trying to build a new EMR, but there were still significant analytic challenges to be addressed. "EHR State of Mind" became an unofficial rallying cry.

Watson Health Offering Management – Fall 2015

"ProjectX is proposed, are there any objections?"

I was listening to a Watson Health Offering Management conference call with my VP of Development. I wasn't officially invited, but he wanted me to hear what was going on. There had to have been at least 50 people on the call.

The proposal was being made by the head of Offering Management. "Offering Management" at IBM is what the rest of the software industry would generally call *Product Management.* I don't even remember what the specific project was, but it was clear that the default answer was Yes and the question was whether anyone wanted to speak up and argue against this decision in front of all the other executives and leaders in Watson Health. This seemed like a bad way to do business. My VP of Development was horrified. Even by IBM standards, this wasn't the way things were supposed to work.

My VP of Development's desk phone, which was on speaker, was now off mute.

"Is there interlock?" he asked.

Interlock? What the hell was that? Although I was normally the one asking uncomfortable questions, I knew enough to keep my mouth shut in this instance. I wasn't even supposed to be on the call.

There was a brief but excruciating pause.

"Is there interlock with development?" he asked again.

Now I got it. Interlock was an IBM term meaning that Offering Management and Development had an agreement, nay, *commitment* for a project, release, or any other activity. Interlock meant there wasn't just an agreement; there was committed capacity. That there were people to actually do the work, and that those people weren't already committed to do something else.

Call it whatever you want, that type of agreement and the underlying trust it represents is the bedrock of effective software development planning and execution. And what had been exposed in that moment was that Watson Health Offering Management was effectively acting like a group of teenagers on a shop till you drop bonanza with borrowed credit cards. *I want this! And that!* My VP of Development wasn't even talking about the merit of the specific proposal, but rather that nobody was seriously thinking about how to operationalize the requests. Who will do the work? Whose budgets are paying for the effort?

This questioning was not appreciated.

That executive meeting was just the tip of the iceberg. The general expectation from Offering Managers was that it was reasonable to go up to any developer and order them to work on something. In an effective software development relationship, there does need to be some flexibility between the product management and engineering functions, but the problem was that it was a complete free-for-all in Offering Management. Every Offering Manager felt empowered to demand things from anybody that was in front of them, and no requests were being rationalized against anybody else's requests, or against reality. Let alone what the existing customer bases wanted.

I had an Offering Manager tell me there should be *two* roadmaps: the things that he wanted and then everything else that engineering wanted, which he called "code hygiene" – a somewhat off-putting phrase that might be funny if he was saying it ironically, but he wasn't. The desire to differentiate between externally and internally driven development tasks is not wrong and is completely reasonable to categorize tickets in Jira in that manner, but there still needed to be **one** roadmap because there was only **one** development team, I tried explaining, pointing at the back room where the team was, without much success. He didn't apparently consider "hygiene" to be his problem as an Offering Manager, even for the products he was managing.

We needed to better explain what Explorys was doing – and just as importantly – *not* doing, and Explorys Engineering created what became known as The Pinwheel of Death in late 2015 to show where resources were being applied. The Pinwheel was a severely sliced up pie chart produced in Excel named in honor of the multicolored spinner that pops up when Macs freeze up, that was kept up to date monthly. While we had a solid team, we were spread extremely thin given the avalanche of requests. I have a Pinwheel from 2017 that showed 101 resources spread across 31 projects.

Worse still, there was *literally* no support for any of the existing acquisition products from Offering Management. All offerings had to be *new* offerings. This produced some unintentionally comic situations where an Offering Manager coming up with a "new" offering idea that was effectively the EPM:Registry functionality Explorys had for years, and insisted that it wasn't anything like Registry because *they* had thought of it, but these moments were only funny in retrospect. They were profoundly frustrating at the time. We had to actively fight with Offering Management to improve the existing portfolio of products.

Even getting the IBM Part Numbers for our products was a challenge. If somebody pulled up to Explorys at this point with a million dollars in a briefcase we couldn't sell them anything without a specified IBM Part Number. Explorys preacquisition did *not* have this problem; trust me, the money would have immediately been taken. In fairness, accurate accounting is important, so the issue wasn't *that* there were Part Numbers, it was *getting* a Part Number into IBM's sellable catalog and figuring out who needed to be arm-wrestled or dance-fought for approval.

Additionally, all acquisition products were to be re-built. Not *extended,* re-built.

Even in late 2015 it was clear – at least to the acquisition companies – that approach was suicidal.

Chapter 7

IBM Watson Health: Stalling

Bluewashing – Spring 2016

This is where Bluewashing really went into overdrive. I started tracking requests for Explorys that were originating from IBMers. The list of IBM people asking us for things was over 30, and that didn't represent *requests* – that number was much higher – those were just the people behind the requests. I could easily have spent every hour of every day just talking with other IBM employees about the IBM products they wanted utilized by Explorys products and solutions.

Aside from marketing reasons for Bluewashing, there were even accounting drivers for it in the form of "green dollars" vs. "blue dollars." Green dollars referred to money received from customers (at least in the United States, where the paper currency is green), and blue dollars were internal IBM credits for product usage inside other IBM products, along with any other IBM accounting and finance magic. IBM Watson Health was a hot division, and everybody at IBM wanted to boost their numbers in any manner available, and as far as everybody

DOI: 10.4324/9781003491590-7

else was concerned, it was a blue dollar land grab. To be perfectly honest, I don't know what the intra-IBM product usage accounting looked like on the books, but I heard the phrases enough times to indicate that there was more to it than just hyperbole.

Data Warehousing

Explorys was using a massively parallel database platform called Vertica for its hosted SuperMart product since 2012, which provided a data warehouse its customers could utilize for custom reporting. Vertica was founded in 2005 as a distributed column-oriented database by renowned database researcher Michael Stonebraker. Vertica wasn't cheap, but it sure was fast, and for its purpose, it was one of the best products on the market. It cannot be overstated just how much IBM hated the fact that we were using Vertica, and this hatred was understandable because IBM had database products of its own. Secondly, because this was a customer-facing product, customers had to configure Vertica JDBC drivers and read the Vertica SQL guide. SuperMart users *knew* they were using Vertica. And they also knew it worked and was very fast. That really fueled IBM's ire. I get it. It wasn't a great look given that Explorys was now under the IBM brand. But like it or not, SuperMart worked. And it needed to keep working for our customers.

The problem was identifying a replacement as IBM had multiple database products. There was Db2, but Db2 didn't work in a scale-out way like Vertica did – we tried testing it. We had requests to start using Netezza for SuperMart, another IBM acquisition from 2010, but Netezza was a data warehouse *appliance* – it was a hardware + software solution. We could have installed some Netezza racks in our Cleveland data center, but we had other people in IBM telling us we needed to get *out* of our Cleveland data center to the Watson Health Cloud and SoftLayer. But Netezza wasn't supported in

SoftLayer at the time, but ironically Vertica – because it was a software-only solution – *could* be deployed there.

It was like trying to navigate a maze where every prospective exit was compromised with some mutually exclusive requirement or trap door. We also were concerned about going through the effort to convert and then having the rug pulled out from under us, in that Netezza might wind up ending up like Informix. Informix was another IBM database acquisition that was eventually sunset.

But when we tried raising concerns, we were again told, "you're at IBM now." And to stop asking so many questions and be easier to deal with.

The Explorys engineering team even tested IBM's BigSQL, a database engine that supported the Hadoop environment, similar to Cloudera's Impala SQL engine and a host of other clones such as Presto, Drill, and SparkSQL. BigSQL performed well, but we kept hearing conflicting stories of whether there was a long-term commitment to the product.

It's not that Explorys was unwilling to change, but the engineering team at least wanted to be close on feature parity, especially given that SuperMart was customer-facing, and if we went through the effort to migrate users and workloads to a new IBM solution, it was a platform that IBM would support going forward.

What would have been appreciated is if the interested IBM product teams were willing to put together test deployments at scale to demonstrate product capabilities, but that's not what happened. All of these meetings and evaluations took time and resources, and the responsibility for response and evaluation was on us. We were guilty until proven IBM.

Storage

Storage proved another telling example. There was a Watson Health Offering Manager who formerly worked with IBM's flash storage products. "Why aren't you using flash storage? You should use flash storage!" he asked/requested/insisted. He liked talking about flash storage, so that became another entry on the list. It was also a typical exchange in that he didn't come prepared with any performance and cost-benefit analysis. He just wanted us to look into the one IBM product that he happened to be familiar with. We were expected to react to the high-level idea and get on it, posthaste, as we were at IBM now.

Then there was IBM's GPFS (General Parallel File System). GPFS is a distributed and redundant file system, and something which we learned would likely be needed to be deployed with Db2 for storage for a full-scale deployment. It is a commercialized product a lot like Hadoops HDFS (Hadoop Distributed File System), but with more bells and whistles. And more expensive.

I also ran into a representative from Cleversafe in early 2016 at an IBM offsite, which was an object storage product that IBM had acquired in November 2015, a few months before. "You're wasting money" he told me. "So much money." His IBM badge was still practically warm from the printer, and we had just met. His disapproval was impressive as it was immediate and total. I'm sure he would do well at IBM.

All three of these IBM storage products had benefits. But determining the *incremental* benefit compared to what Explorys already had was the hard part, and at what cost. Just as the with SuperMart and trying to replace Vertica it wasn't just about operating costs, the conversion process itself also had costs.

Again, Explorys was presumed guilty until proven IBM, even if it wasn't clear what that meant.

Although object storage would become the default storage platform for data warehousing in public cloud computing in the coming years with S3 in AWS, ADLS Gen2 in Azure, and Google Storage in Google Cloud, the issue was our current context. We could deploy Cleversafe in our Cleveland

Data Center, but we were already using Hadoop and HDFS for our data storage in multiple clusters, and those clusters were already running on commodity hardware. HDFS and Cleversafe both employed data replication to protect against server loss and other failures, but even if Cleversafe might somehow have had incrementally more cost-efficient storage (which was the claim), HDFS supported directory structures but Cleversafe did not. This means that converting to Cleversafe was anything than a 1:1 swap and would take significant retooling in our workflows. Not impossible, of course, but again – for what benefit and what cost?

And all of that was predicated on installing Cleversafe in the Cleveland Data Center, which was not being encouraged. But the situation with SoftLayer was even less clear at the time. And that would mean bringing the rest of the Explorys stack along for the ride, which was an even larger project.

IBM did, however, have a Hadoop distribution called IOP, so at least we could make somebody happy. Explorys upgraded its Data Lake cluster to IOP in 2017, and then IBM promptly killed that product. Thanks for nothing.

That Unfocused Feeling

Even by the beginning of 2016 we could feel Explorys slipping. Operationally we were still moving forward from the pre-acquisition momentum but from a product management standpoint we were already starting to bleed out. The Chilmark February 2016 review of IBM Watson Health – and specifically Explorys – was alarming:

> ***Explorys is strong in product capabilities but does not score high for market vision. This is in part due to Explorys becoming part of Watson Health***. *The top three differentiators noted:*
>
> - Promise of IBM Watson technology

- Known HIT brands with Explorys and Phytel
- *True big data implementation*

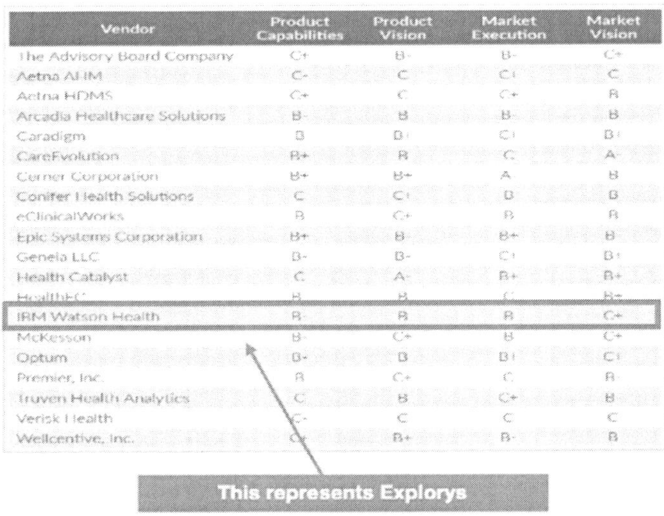

Vendor	Product Capabilities	Product Vision	Market Execution	Market Vision
The Advisory Board Company	C+	B-	B-	C+
Aetna AHM	C-	C	C+	C
Aetna HDMS	C+	C	C+	B
Arcadia Healthcare Solutions	B-	B	B-	B
Caradigm	B	B+	C+	B+
CareEvolution	B+	B	C	A-
Cerner Corporation	B+	B+	A	B
Conifer Health Solutions	C	C+	B	B
eClinicalWorks	B	C+	B	B
Epic Systems Corporation	B+	B	B+	B
Genela LLC	B-	B-	C+	B+
Health Catalyst	C	A-	B+	B+
HealthEC	B	B	C	B+
IBM Watson Health	B-	B	B	C+
McKesson	B-	C+	B	C+
Optum	B-	B	B+	C+
Premier, Inc.	B	C+	C	B-
Truven Health Analytics	C	B	C+	B
Verisk Health	C-	C	C	C
Wellcentive, Inc.	C+	B+	B-	B

Figure 7.1 Chilmark – February 2016. IBM Watson Health in this chart was effectively Explorys and Phytel. The green annotations are from the author, not the original Chilmark chart. Note: Chilmark Research ceased operations in 2024.

Talk about a direct hit: strong capabilities, and a lot of potential, but lack of market vision. This review came about ten months of Explorys being acquired by IBM, and two months before Watson Health acquired Truven.

This was alarming. Rather, this *should* have been alarming if anyone in leadership were paying attention.

SoftLayer

Explorys got to know SoftLayer and Watson Health Cloud, the cloud infrastructure that Watson Health was building on it, all too well.

As previously mentioned, SoftLayer was itself an IBM acquisition in 2013, less than two years before Watson Health was established. Its primary target market was relatively small-footprint hosted solutions, such as a website/database technical stack consisting of perhaps a half-dozen servers. It wasn't known for cloud-native solutions and programmable infrastructure-as-a-service like public clouds AWS, Azure, and GCP. SoftLayer was effectively a cloud-based commercial data center like we were already deployed in, although without the option of high-end networking and extensibility which we needed. Different, but not really better, and in more than a few ways, worse. And more expensive. A lot more expensive. And to make matters worse, we were supposed to deploy through the Watson Health Cloud, a layer on top of SoftLayer. This required working through a human for approval to deploy. A guy. A single person. It was the opposite of modern DevOps, and the practices already in place in Cleveland.

Our DevOps team did an extensive analysis factoring in everything – recurring costs such as power, cooling, floor-space, network maintenance, personnel, and one-time costs such as core network hardware, racks, and network hardware – and determined that SoftLayer, even without the Watson Health Cloud overhead, was 3.5 times more expensive on a per-rack basis than our current infrastructure. Not 3.5% more expensive. Not 35% more expensive. *3.5 times* more expensive. Running on SoftLayer was going to come out of our budget, and Explorys was expected to gladly accept these additional costs as a part of our operating expenses. It would have been an eight-figure budget impact. We were supposed to accept this and say Thank You.

SoftLayer *was* an IBM acquisition, but it was also IBM mostly and kind of. The prices that SoftLayer was charging IBM were the same prices that it was charging the public. Nobody at IBM seemed to have studied the concepts of transfer pricing. After about a year of raising this issue, the Watson

Health Cloud division used the Explorys analysis to negotiate a discount for themselves, which was funny. The renegotiated price was now "only" 2.3 times as expensive as Explorys' infrastructure.

This was not an argument against cloud infrastructure in general; rather, it was about finding the *right* cloud. Explorys started in a commercial data center because there wasn't any other option at the time, especially one that its healthcare customers would trust and could safely handle HIPAA workloads. As the technology landscape changed, Explorys could have benefited from the flexibility of public cloud architecture, but fundamentally, SoftLayer was the wrong platform as it just wasn't in the same class as other options. It would have still taken a lot of effort to convert Explorys' solutions to a cloud-native architecture, but it would have been *possible* had we had the right platform to target. All the hours spent talking about SoftLayer were another dead end, and another drain on our time.

The Big Legal World of IBM

"IP (Intellectual Property) harvesting" is when the IBM lawyers come around acquisitions looking for things to patent.

Patents are one of those subjects that people either care a lot about or they don't think about at all. IBM loves patents and dedicates a lot of time and money to the process. The harvesting started for Explorys in Summer 2015 just after acquisition.

We had a lawyer stop by to meet our senior engineering folks to tell us how important patents were to IBM, how the patent process in terms of what was generally patentable and what wasn't, and the differences between United States (must be filed within 12 months of first public usage or disclosure) and European Patents (must be filed before first public usage or disclosure), and that the patent process was very important to IBM, just in case we had missed it the first time. He also stressed not to limit our thinking and just concentrate on generating ideas. "Don't try to be the lawyer, that's my job." That sounded reasonable. We could get behind that.

A week or two later, an IBM Lawyer and outside counsel came back for a harvesting/idea-generating session. I couldn't make it because I had to travel somewhere for work, probably to New York for one of many meetings to talk about the proposed Watson Health Cloud. But I know what happened because my phone immediately blew up with instant messages. An Explorys executive had shown up to the Explorys engineering IP harvesting and was arguing *against* all the engineering patent ideas. None of our work was patentable, according to the Explorys executive. I had multiple engineers telling me the exact same story.

We had all seen this behavior before, and escalating this was not going to achieve much.

> *"and the three men brought Explorys to life."*

I was going to have to take care of it myself.

I called the IBM Lawyer the next day and told him that I had multiple engineers telling me the exact same story, that an Explorys executive was arguing against the engineering patents, which was precisely what were told *not* to do during this process. I asked the IBM Lawyer to describe what he saw and heard in that meeting.

There was a long silence on the other end of the phone. The lawyer had said enough.

I told the lawyer that it should have been clear from the initial meeting that Explorys engineering was supportive of the IBM IP harvesting process. But if IBM Legal wanted to keep working with the engineering team he had to keep working directly with Explorys engineering and keep any other

Explorys executives out of the patent process, otherwise this wasn't going to work. I had only been a part of IBM for a couple of months at that point and I probably should have gone to the IBM Integration Executive with this, but somebody had to say it.

The lawyer agreed. After that, things moved along fine.

I was issued four patents from my time at IBM. IBM's innovation process is probably typical of other large corporations in that there are "innovation points" granted per patent application per inventor, and then a few more points and a certificate suitable for framing are granted in the event a patent is issued. There is a small amount of money attached (~$1,500 for application, ~$750 for issue, or there abouts) as well. There are "innovation plateaus" that come with small bonuses, and another certificate suitable for framing. My patent collection is small potatoes compared to people from IBM Research who might accumulate 50 or 100 patents or more. From a corporate perspective, though, it's rarely about a single patent but rather a portfolio of patents. It's about building a shield-wall of intellectual property. Or a bludgeon. Or both.

I was a co-inventor on a patent application that Explorys filed long before it was acquired. That application worked its way through the system for a few more years, but it was eventually issued while I was still at IBM. Even though I was an IBM employee and IBM was now the holder of that patent, IBM would not award any "innovation points" – the rationale being that it was not invented "on IBM time." This denial seemed overly and humorously cheap given that there was so little at stake for the co-inventors at this point besides a few hundred dollars and another certificate suitable for framing. Such is life in the corporate innovation game.

I never had to get involved in lawsuits with respect to patent defense, and those can get particularly ugly. I did get exposed to another legal battle though. Explorys and other Watson Health units were named in a broad lawsuit aimed at

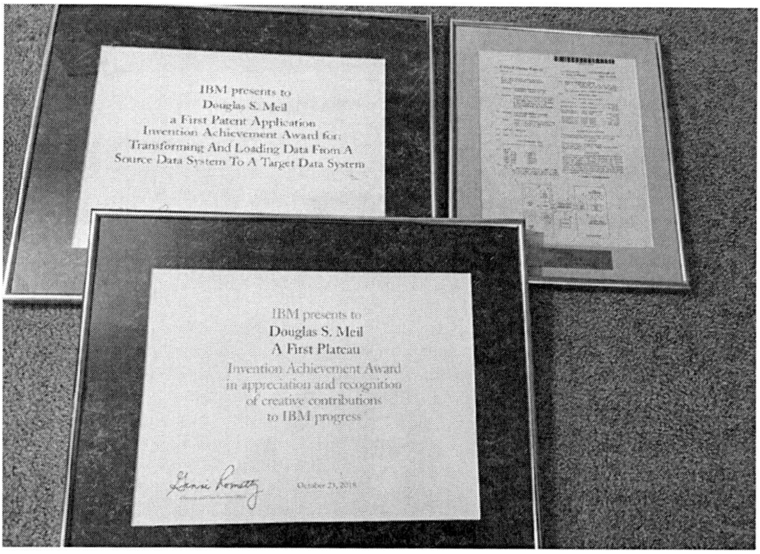

Figure 7.2 IBM innovation certificates suitable for framing.

IBM. As was explained to me, the complaint originated from a company that had once worked with IBM on a project, but the business relationship had run its course, and it wasn't apparently an amicable breakup. This company was claiming that IBM had taken their technology and was utilizing it in other efforts outside the original contracted scope. If that were true, that would indeed be bad, but our unit had never heard of this company, so there was no way we could have appropriated said technology. Somebody still had to go on the record and say that, so this is where I had to learn how to get deposed in a lawsuit.

I had to fly to Manhattan and head to a fancy legal office, just like on TV. I was seated at the head of a rectangular table and across from me was a video camera and operator. At my left elbow was a court stenographer. On the left side of the table was opposing counsel, and on the right side was the counsel representing my company. I had to be sworn in. "This is just like TV," I thought. Getting deposed is a life experience, however, like being almost mauled by a tiger or seeing a tornado far too up-close, which sounds cooler than it really is. Fortunately, I was prepared by IBM Legal.

The essential preparatory lessons were:

- Answer the question that was asked. If somebody asks you about lunch on Wednesday, don't offer details about breakfast and dinner, much less describe the menu for Tuesday and Thursday
- If confused, ask to speak to counsel. Invoke the phrase "I need to speak to counsel," just like on TV
- Don't write anything down. This can be tricky for habitual note-takers, as writing something down during a legal deposition is the same thing as saying it out loud

I had to answer "No" or "No, that is not correct" for about two hours of questioning from opposing counsel, and that fortunately concluded my involvement in the litigation response.

While I consider myself lucky to have multiple patents, I would be content with the deposition experience being a one-and-done.

Watson

> In part, he says, IBM is suffering from its ambition: It was the first company to make a major push to bring AI to the clinic. But it also earned ill will and skepticism by boasting of Watson's abilities. "They came in with marketing first, product second, and got everybody excited."
>
> **IEEE Spectrum (April 2, 2019)**

When attending big data conferences during this period, one could hear major tech companies talk about AI and machine learning projects with a fairly standard vocabulary: unsupervised and supervised learning, clustering algorithms, classifiers, and regression algorithms. But IBM had *Cognitive Computing*. Huh? What?? That approach had contrasting effects: technical people didn't take Watson seriously, and business people took Watson *too* seriously, causing inflated and unrealistic expectations. Admittedly, in 2024 saying something is "cognitive" has gotten trendier because of generative AI and Large Language Models, but in 2015 the phrase was confounding.

On top of that, IBM tried at the time to tie Watson to a variety of other IBM products, like only running on IBM hardware, or only being available on the IBM Cloud. Watson was not just confusingly described, but its intelligence was artificially limited. Watson never really factored into any serious product conversations at Explorys, but it's not like we were trying to avoid it. Acquisitions still running on their existing hosting infrastructure, such as Explorys, couldn't easily take advantage of Watson – whatever it was – even if they wanted to.

I give IBM a lot of credit for its Deep Blue Chess projects and its Jeopardy effort. That was some innovative and out-of-the-box thinking. I will freely admit to having my picture taken by the Jeopardy game podium at the Yorktown Heights Research Center. I even had a member of the Jeopardy team perform a fantastic guest talk at the tech meetup I ran (Cleveland Big Data Meetup). Like I said, I'm a fan of those efforts. IBM demonstrated a remarkable level of flexibility in its Jeopardy effort by embracing a significant portion of open-source software in its construction, and it also demonstrated patience because it took a lot of work and a lot of iteration to make Jeopardy a success. But IBM lost its way on Watson by focusing on magic instead of technical excellence. Big sales. Quick bucks. Now. Years later, IBM relabeled Cognitive Computing as something else, and even later started supporting Watson on non-IBM cloud platforms like Azure and AWS (heresy of the highest order during my time at IBM), but the damage was done as far as Watson Health was concerned. It was another lost opportunity.

Bluewashing – Summer 2016

Product Integration

One development effort that was proceeding, albeit painfully, was the product integration between Explorys and Watson Care Manager (WCM). The business and clinical case made broad sense to integrate a population analytic platform and a care management solution. Explorys calculates care gaps and identifies risk areas. WCM was used for patient follow-up by the care management teams. So far so good. The technical approach taken made much less sense, though.

What Explorys advocated from the start was a lightweight approach for patient referrals from system to system, and where Explorys' Virtual Chart could be windowed into the Watson Care Manager experience for as seamless as experience as possible under the circumstances. This approach had the advantage of a minimizing data transfer and other moving pieces, which was not a small detail given the number of datatypes in the chart, plus it leveraged the user interface from Explorys. This approach was immediately actionable, and we could get it up and running quickly.

What the WCM team wanted was a different approach. They wanted all the clinical data for referred patients transferred and resident in their system. And with record-level updates, because a healthcare data was stateful and could be modified. The result was a far more heavyweight integration that took a long time to work the kinks out and wound up making no-one happy, especially the customers.

For starters, WCM was designed for care management on configured forms that were entered by humans. The WCM engineers had completely underestimated what it meant to send along all the clinical data, especially for patients that need care management, which tend to be sick had a sizable medical history. The initial volume of data blew up their application. Throwing thousands of lab tests at them – or worse – for example, forced WCM to resolve user-interface design and usability issues that Explorys had addressed years earlier.

Another one of the other battles was how to transfer to the data to WCM. Explorys was using Apache Kafka for messaging, but the Watson Health Cloud was insisting data be transferred with IBM's Integration Bus (IIB) framework over IBM's MQ messaging product. This was systems design not just by committee but also with a dozen backseat drivers to boot and agonizing to remember that the primary use-case was for the users to see the Explorys Virtual Chart for clinical data. A virtual chart which already existed.

Adding further complexity was the fact that WCM was hosted on the Watson Health Cloud on SoftLayer. There was a lot of manual environment administration added with Watson Health Cloud, and the WCM developers had extremely limited access to debug when things went wrong. Which naturally, they did frequently. There were absolute heroics on the Explorys side to debug the WCM environment.

As simple as this integration sounds it took many months to build and coordinate testing, and many months to stabilize. The overall effort limped along for probably two years, with underwhelming results typically for things beyond Explorys' control, such as WCM outages.

I was at a customer meeting in Spring 2018 about Explorys/WCM integration. They were polite and appreciated the efforts in getting this integration to work, but we also found out that this customer was dumping both Explorys and WCM for another product that had an integrated solution for both functions. The original approach was really what they wanted. They just wanted to see the chart. This isn't an argument against API-based integration in general, of course, but a lesson in considering what users not just wanted but needed.

Managing the Pinwheel

I had 18 business trips in 2016. For sales and account managers professionals this doesn't seem like much, but for an engineer this was a lot. Nearly all of those business trips were to other IBM facilities trying to fight fires. The Pinwheel of Death was getting worse. Explorys was bombarded with requests but they were overwhelmingly of the Bluewash variety and not things that would benefit our customers. There was still no awareness of Chilmark's "lack of market vision" assessment earlier in the year within Watson Health leadership.

In the Summer of 2016 my VP of Development and I flew to an impromptu offsite to meet with Phytel to scope out a product integration approach on our own because this still seemed like an obvious customer need, and this integration was still not on any official product roadmap. Our meeting was entirely unauthorized by Offering Management.

If Explorys was going to be saved, engineering was going to have to try and grab the steering wheel.

Cleveland Cavaliers – Summer 2016

Midwest rust-belt cities experienced economic hard times before the rest of the country when manufacturing first started moved to the southern United States in the 1960s, and then overseas. Cleveland is one such city. A big reason Bruce Springsteen had such a dedicated fan base in the area is because when he sang about mills closing and people being down and out, those things were actually happening to Clevelanders – it wasn't just art. But at least rust-belt cities could take solace in the success of their sports teams. Pittsburgh, for example, had great success in baseball and football in the 1970s.

But not Cleveland.

Cleveland had not won a major sports championship since the 1964 Browns in the pre-Super Bowl era. The Browns had a habit of almost doing something amazing and then failing in some equally and uniquely catastrophic Cleveland way. Red Right 88, the Drive, and the Fumble are stories that every Browns fan knows by heart. The Indians – as they were known at the time – were very nearly as bad when there were satirized in the film *Major League*. But they had better luck and made the World Series twice in the 1990s (1995 and 1997), with the 1997 loss coming in a devastating Cleveland-esque game seven collapse in the 9th inning. The Cavaliers made it to the NBA Finals in 2007 but were blown out. They made the finals again in 2015 and made a more respectable showing but still came up short.

Cleveland just couldn't seem to get over the championship threshold. Almost, but not quite.

It was June 2016, and the Cavaliers were back in the NBA Finals. Two years in a row? Thrice in a decade? Some cities could get spoiled with results like this. Not Cleveland.

The Cavaliers were blown out in the first two games of the series and then found themselves down three games to one. Fans could at least take solace in that they didn't get shut out in the finals like 2007. The Golden State Warriors were a terrific team.

Then the unthinkable happened. For the first time in NBA history a team came back from a three-games-to-one deficit to win. The Cavaliers were NBA champions, and Cleveland has its first major sports championship in over 50 years. Cleveland celebrated with a parade with a million people in attendance. An actual *one million people*.

Cleveland was finally a winner! The feeling was everywhere.

Anything was possible, right? Even at IBM?

Hope is a dangerous thing.

Chapter 8

IBM Distinguished

Becoming a Distinguished Engineer

Being named an IBM Fellow is the top technical honor that an IBM employee can aspire to. IBM started naming Fellows in 1963, and the list includes names like Backus, Amdahl, Mandelbrot, Codd, and many others. Anyone not familiar with those names should be. The list of IBM Fellows includes Nobel Prize winners and Association for Computing Machinery (ACM) Turing Award winners, which is effectively the Nobel Prize in computing. The ACM and Institute of Electrical and Electronics Engineers (IEEE) have Fellows. Google and Microsoft have some Fellows. I would hazard a guess that every company in the tech sector that has honorifics has in some way modeled their programs on IBM. IBM probably borrowed the *Fellows* concept from somewhere else, like the Royal Society in the United Kingdom, but that is a story for another time.

Becoming a Fellow is a big deal because only a handful are appointed each year, and the appointment is approved by the CEO of IBM, and a Fellow is an *executive appointment.* Being an executive is a big deal at IBM. Job-bands at IBM range from one to ten, with six to ten being the professional-grade bands.

DOI: 10.4324/9781003491590-8

Executive bands start at D, then go to C, B, and A. Becoming an executive is when you cross the boundary from a Band 10 to a D. There is a world of difference between those levels. Even a C-grade executive at IBM is a big muckity-muck. An A-grade executive would probably be a general manager of a division. Rumor had it that executive grades went even higher for IBM SVPs and the CEO, perhaps "AA" or other unpronounceable Unicode glyphs. As it was described to me, an appointment to Fellow meant a D-level executive appointment.

At some point in its history, IBM realized that it needed to add a few more, but lower, brass rings to reach for, and as far as I could tell it happened in the 1990s. Those rings were Senior Member of Technical Staff (STSM) and Distinguished Engineer (DE). An STSM is an appointment that can be granted to a Band 10 employee, so in a sense they are a "Band 10+." Extra special. STSM appointments can be granted by a committee within an employee's division, after the candidate submits a proposal package, probably not unlike the process of submitting for academic tenure. A DE is a D-grade *corporate* executive appointment similar to a Fellow that requires all the paperwork that an STSM requires, plus the multi-step high-level approval drama that a Fellow requires. A DE appointment requires the eventual approval by the #2 person in IBM.

It cannot be stressed enough that while much is expected of candidates in this process, they are *pulled up* to these levels. This doesn't happen on your own. You don't apply by yourself. Executives literally need to lobby for you. I was fortunate to have a Technical Executive who not just supported me but also had been at IBM for years and knew the ropes.

The Package

Package writing is an art, and fortunately, I received good counsel on how to assemble it. There are three sections that are equally important:

- Candidate's accomplishments
- The proposed role
- Executive endorsements

I got a tap on the shoulder to start preparing a package "just in case" in late 2015 by my VP of Development, with support from Explorys' Integration Executive. Both put me in touch with other DEs who knew this process worked. Again, just in case. Given when I was assembling the material, just about everything in the package was about my work at Explorys, the Apache HBase project, and the Cleveland Big Data Meetup.

The next part to prepare was the proposed role. The phrase "appointment" is key because as important as historical accomplishments are, defining the future responsibilities is just as important. This is more than an award. It is a new *role*. This is how a newly minted STSM, DE, or Fellow will represent IBM going forward.

Once a draft role was agreed upon between my VP of Development, the Integration Executive, and me, it was time to get shopped around. Literally. I was trotted out for conversations with other DEs and other IBM executives to see if I was IBM executive material. I did a few presentations and was peppered with questions.

Then I was introduced to the fine art of IBM executive endorsements. This required a level of plotting, back-channeling, and discretion that approached a State Department negotiation. It's very much who you know and the real work happens on the down-low.

First, my VP of Development would make an inquiry to another executive regarding support for the general idea of my candidacy. I would then ghost-write endorsement quotes and submit them to the executive for approval. The quotes would typically take the form of:

> Doug would represent IBM well because … <fill in blank> .

I would then learn as much as I could about the executive and the products and services they support and write a version of how I would support them. For example, let's say that a particular executive valued TechnologyX. I would submit something like this for them to review:

> Doug would represent IBM well because he has a solid understanding of TechnologyX and will provide technical leadership for IBM's TechnologyX initiatives.

If they liked it, then it was added to the package as:

> Doug would represent IBM well because he a solid understanding of TechnologyX and will provide technical leadership for IBM's TechnologyX initiatives. – TJ Watson, JR.

My package was about 35 pages when it was all said and done. Most of it was accomplishments, which is typical. But without the other two sections the package would be dead on arrival.

The Role

Through speaking with other executives, DEs, and Fellows, I learned a lot about technical leadership at IBM. Some of them had been in their roles for a few years, and some had been in technical leadership for quite some time. It was interesting mix of perspectives and history. A common theme was that DEs were supposed to act like "knights on a chessboard." That phrasing and it appealed to me. DEs were supposed to be driving solutions and help solve problems, jumping over things when necessary, and expected to seek opportunities for IBM. DEs were *not* supposed to be lane-stayers. If all else failed, DEs were supposed to be the people that could be trusted to tell executives what was really going on. It could take multiple years to really settle into a DE role, not just because of the corporate product portfolio but the relationship-building across divisions. There was much to learn about being an effective Technical Executive, but I was eager for the challenge.

The Pitch

My VP of Development presented my package to the divisional board in April 2016. In addition to the package, I had to prepare a short presentation about myself. I was not present at this meeting. No candidate is.

I was told that the result was positive and that the powers that be had thought it worthy of consideration for a DE appointment. Then it went to corporate. There needed to be a budgetary review for the appointment, and then another corporate review. At this point the process could be slowed down or halted, but nothing could speed it up. It was not only out of my hands, it was also out of my VP of Development's hands.

While I couldn't *entirely* forget about it, I had shove this in the back corner of my mind and get on with other more pressing matters.

The Announcement

No part of this story was entirely normal, so the DE announcement was destined not to be as well.

Jump-cut to Monday September 12, 2016. I had *mostly* forgotten about the DE process because there wasn't anything I could do about it. I was organizing not just another Cleveland Big Data Meetup, but a Mega Meetup. This was the annual blowout where the group rented something big, and this year it was the Cleveland Museum of Natural History. There were over 400 people RSVP'd to the meetup, and as any meetup organizer knows you never get 100% attendance but there had to be close to 300 people who showed-up. This was a legit nerd party.

I had invited *Cleveland Scene*, a local alternative newspaper, to the event for some press coverage. A September 12, 2016, article titled "Night at the Museum … for Cleveland's Robust Big Data Community" described the somewhat bizarre scene witnessed by the attending reporter:

> Before the evening's presentations in the Murch Auditorium, Meil's co-worker Steve McHale, CEO and co-founder of IBM's Explorys, grabbed the microphone and announced that Meil had been awarded a coveted distinction in the IBM community, in fact the company's second-highest honor for engineers. McHale went on to say that the success of the Big Data Meet Up was attributable largely to Meil's enthusiasm and dogged coordination. Meil smiled and thanked the applauding crowd quickly. "Now back to our regularly scheduled programming," he said.

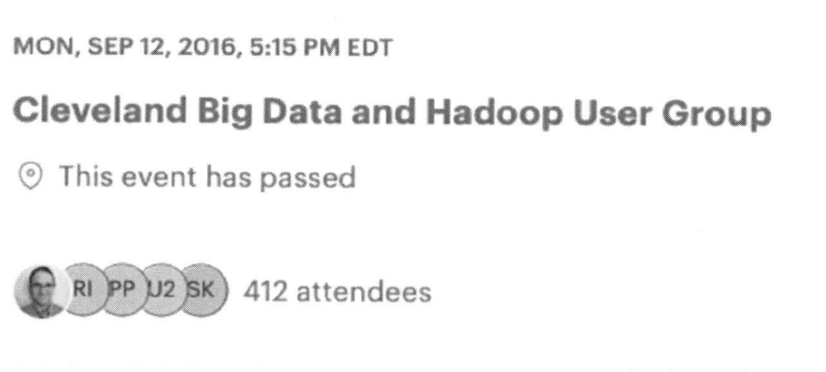

Figure 8.1 Cleveland Big Data Mega Meetup September 2016, with over 400 RSVPs. https://www.meetup.com/cleveland-hadoop/events/228560668/

Figure 8.2 Cleveland Museum of Natural History's then-director Dr Evalyn Gates, second from right.

That is how I found out that I had been appointed an IBM Distinguished Engineer. While I certainly was happy for the news, becoming a DE was the last thing on my mind at that moment. I had been preparing for this meetup for months as a nights and weekends hobby, and there were hundreds of people in the audience and six presentations to get through. There were several attributes the meetup was known for, such as everybody getting fed and everybody getting thanked. Another was that the meetup started on time and ended on time. I used a cheap kitchen timer to keep things running. When I advertised "20 minute slots" I really meant it. *Twenty. Minutes.* It was disrespectful to the audience and speakers to do otherwise.

While IBM was a sponsor of the event, which I appreciated, it was a *minor* sponsor. As with all the other Cleveland Big Data Meetup events, the vast majority of the sponsor money came from the broader technical community, which I had to coordinate and implement in a nice-but-on-the-cheap manner to keep costs low. It was the startup mentality applied to technical event organizing.

When McHale walked on the stage as reported in the article, I was not just looking at someone who wasn't on the meetup agenda. I was also looking at someone who for years had been telling a creation story of Explorys that was in direct opposition to the accomplishments that had been documented in my now-approved DE package. My DE package said, as described in this book, that I had led the design and implementation of Explorys' product portfolio from the inception of the company. I had been at Explorys full-time since the skunkworks. But I was never included in the creation story, nor was Explorys engineering.

"and the three men brought Explorys to life."

While it does take a community to make a successful meetup, I had in fact founded the meetup and been organizing it for the past six years. McHale's comment that I was "largely attributable" for the meetup's success was oddly legalistic, as if he had been advised by his personal attorney not to use words like "creator" and "founder" around me, was a cherry on top. I was also looking at someone who was "value-negging" the meetup the prior year. The pattern would generally go as follows: Dr Jain would complain to McHale about "what is the value of X?" It could be a thing or a person. Anything. Then after getting sufficiently wound up – which didn't take much - McHale would go around asking "what is the value of X?" and then that would become the emergency of the day and a response would need to be scrabbled together. Engineers referred to this behavior in many ways, the most common being *The Eye of Sauron,* and it was a constant source of instability within Explorys. So when McHale and Dr Jain asked me "what is the value of the meetup?" independently within 24 hours the prior year, I could see what was happening. It was an odd question given that I had been running the meetup for almost five years at that point, but I still replied that it was useful as a recruiting tool and to keep tabs on what was happening in the industry. They could have each asked me about what the latest *topics* or *trends* were, but that wasn't what they asked. They asked about the *value* of the meetup, which they might have seen for themselves if either had attended one, but they had not. McHale's one and only appearance was at that Mega Meetup, and Dr Jain never attended.

I was standing on stage in front of a large crowd in a very strange headspace, and the reporter clearly caught the awkward vibe. I paused for a second and really did say "Now back to our regularly scheduled programming," as described in the article. The meetup got back on track and went to plan.

I would have preferred McHale make the DE announcement *at work*, as being appointed a DE was an IBM thing. But

Figure 8.3 Author with IBM Distinguished Engineer celebration cakes.

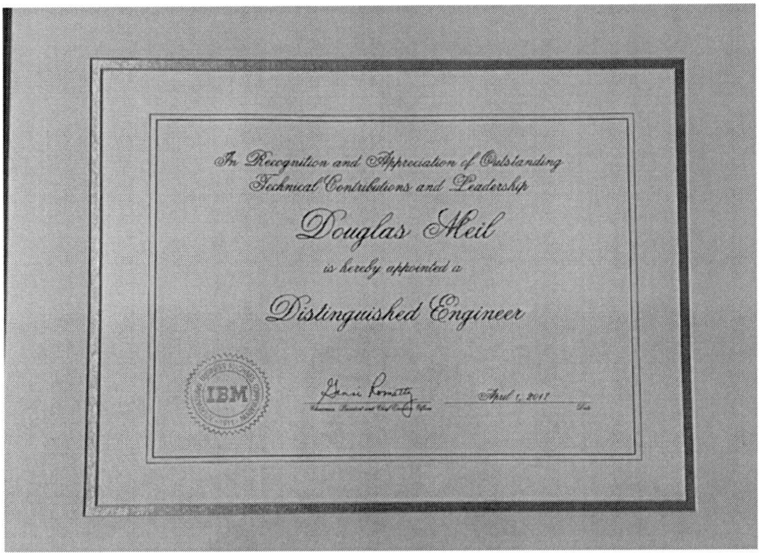

Figure 8.4 Say what you want about IBM, but I did receive several fancy certificates suitable for framing.

that was not the path taken because it would have risked contradicting the Explorys creation story, especially if said in front of Dr Jain. That full-company announcement never happened.

There was a proper work celebration, however. My VP of Development got cookie cakes for the engineering team. I was touched and humbled by the gesture, and thankful for everybody that supported me in the process. That list was long.

At the time of the appointment in September 2016, I would have been happy to keep supporting Explorys and IBM for the rest of my career.

Chapter 9

IBM Watson Health: Decline

Value-Based Care Reorg – Fall 2016

By the late Summer 2016 it was becoming clear enough that Watson Health as a division was failing the acquisition companies. There was a reorganization within Watson Health of a Value-Based Care unit with Explorys, Phytel, and the recently acquired Truven. On paper, this was a reasonable idea as Truven was known primarily for claims analytics. There was potential in this approach.

Unfortunately, this presented a new set of challenges. Truven had been owned by a private equity company for the prior seven years and operated on severe cost controls because it had been restructured to sell. The development team was 55–60% offshore contractors. There were stories of innovative projects from years past, but the names on the PowerPoint proposals tended to be of former employees. The Truven Technical Executive had a reputation as a beat-down manager.

DOI: 10.4324/9781003491590-9

From a business standpoint, Truven had been around for decades and had stable, if slightly declining, numbers. But trying to mix Explorys into this was a cultural disaster. The pattern of internally focused conversations continued but was now focused on Truven.

The Truven Technical Executive insisted on skip-level meetings with some Explorys software engineers, so neither I nor my VP of Development was in the room. This meeting pattern isn't crazy and can be useful for improving direct communication with leadership. The Explorys engineers emerged from the skip-level horrified. It took a long conversation to talk everybody off the ledge.

In our debriefing of the skip-level, we quickly understood why. They had asked the Truven Technical Executive what was going to happen to stem emerging customer losses. The answer was blunt: "we'll get new customers." While the sentiment was admirable on its face, it showed no awareness of the market reality and the disconnect with Offering Management. The Technical Executive's statement "our job is to get the money from our customers pockets and put it in our shareholder's pockets" complete with hand movements moving a dollar from one pocket to the other, didn't help either. Talk about saying the quiet part out loud. Business development *was* important, which is why the Explorys software engineers were asking about customer retention and growth, but that answer was both shocking and crass to the ears of people that got into healthcare to improve patient care. It's pretty much exactly what you would expect from an executive from a company owned by private equity.

Conversations about consolidating technical architecture within Value-Based Care (VBC) acquisitions were excruciating. "Why should I have more than one Hadoop cluster?" he asked. Even Explorys had more than one cluster, and we were more than happy to explain why if he would stop and listen, which he wasn't interested in doing. But properly answering the question that was best done in the context of the overall product portfolio, such as the products we were trying to bring to market in support of our customers. And we weren't having those conversations.

These were yet more examples of Chilmark's "lack of market vision" assessment earlier in the year.

In attempt to make customer data onboarding faster, the Truven Technical Executive also displayed a disconcerting lack of understanding of healthcare data by saying that we should not accept data that "wasn't clean." Truven was largely known for claims analytics, and while certainly not simple, the data integration process is performed through 837 (billing), 835 (remit), and eligibility file transfers. Because the claims process affects eventual payment, there is some necessary standardization in the process. Explorys was primarily known for *clinical* data analytics, and the clinical side of data management is far more open-ended about what and how things are recorded. Doctors and nurses are going to type what doctors and nurses are going to type. Downstream analytics vendors weren't really in a position to tell their healthcare customers what to enter and what not to enter in their electronic medical records, at least if they wanted to deliver any analytic products. Any analytic vendor that was waiting for *perfectly clean data* from a healthcare organization was going to be waiting a long time. But that was the Technical Executive's guidance: just tell our healthcare customers to send us clean data.

It was exasperating.

When the Truven Technical Executive asked about our recruiting strategy, we explained it. We were building up talent year over year, with an eye for multi-year involvement of products. We explained the importance of college recruiting and technical community involvement. He replied with a hostile and arguably unhinged retort, "you think you're better than me?" and then stated that offshoring with contractors was the way it was going to be.

It wasn't just that he didn't listen, it was *how* he didn't listen.

We could hardly have been more un-aligned.

Such interactions weren't IBM's fault, as IBM didn't create Truven. But they became IBM's problem. And became Explorys' latest leadership nightmare.

When It Rains – 2017

It was January 2017, and although his body was failing, his mind was still pretty much there. It had been a tough 18 prior months watching him slide. He was nearing the end of his life, but my dad could see it on my face. I hadn't tried talking about work much with him because I didn't want to add to his stress. But it was all over me. He could see it. Sense it.

> "You look tired."

And that from a dying man. Damn. That is not what I wanted to hear.

> "Just working through a chaotic situation at work" I told him. "We'll see what happens."

Indeed. There wasn't much else to say.

A few more weeks went by and my mom got the call from hospice on Wednesday afternoon February 1, 2017 that it was time. It might be hours, days, or weeks, but it's coming. I took off Thursday and Friday and spent the next four days at the nursing home.

If there was any part of him left, I know he would worry about leaving his family behind. I told him that he could go, and that I was going to be ok. I figured that's what he would want to hear if he could still hear me. They were the hardest words I've ever said.

I saw him Monday morning and then to work. A co-worker who knew what was going on was surprised to see me at work given that the hospice situation was still ongoing. I told him that I just had four straight days of bedside vigil and I felt like I had enough. I just couldn't take any more. I was going continue to see him before and after work.

Monday evening. "You can go, I am going to be ok" I said.

Tuesday morning. "You can go, I am going to be ok" I said.

The hospice team had been immensely supportive. They had little rolling comfort crash carts of snacks and tea, ready to be deployed at a moment's notice in the facility. Hospice is as much for the grieving family as it is for the soon to be deceased. They explained the process as best they could do and emphasized not to try to *catch* death or feel like if we weren't there at the very end that efforts were in vain. Just do your best to say your goodbyes.

As I was driving to him after work on Tuesday, I got a call from my sister when I was about 15 minutes out. As hospice likes to say, he crossed over. He passed. I was minutes from seeing him once more but through the hospice coaching, I knew it was time. It doesn't make it less sad, though.

He had signed up for the Cleveland Clinic Body Donation program years before. It was his idea. Even in death, if there was one more chance to push healthcare, science, and humanity forward, he would take it. I thought it was an amazing example to set. Progress is sometimes made in leaps and bounds but it happens far more often in tiny steps whether they be participating in a clinical trial, relaying the most seemingly minor of clinical feedback, or someone letting their body be used to teach the next generation of medical professionals. For those that don't know, dead bodies are used in medical school anatomy labs. Chopped up, dissected, and studied. It might smell bad and look scary, but it is how the process works. Powered by small anonymous sacrifices.

My dad the teaching cadaver. It made me smile. It would make him smile too.

Death is a part of life. Death is a part of healthcare too.

Selah.

I took a deep breath went back to work. There had to be some way for us to make a small dent in healthcare. Hopefully Watson Health wasn't also running out of time.

Disorganizational Structure – 2017

A clarifying aspect of a startup is that people typically know things are either *all* going to work or *all* going to fail. A ship doesn't *half*-crash onto the rocks, for example, and remain sail-worthy. With effective leadership this type of existential challenge can be channeled into a coherent and energizing mission. Explorys had its leadership issues but in general the engineering team fully internalized this dynamic and designed and acted accordingly, which is why the Provider solutions and Secondary Use solutions were built in a unified architecture and supported by mostly coordinated teams.

After the Watson Health Value-Based Care (VBC) reorganization, the Explorys Provider products and Explorys Secondary Use products were split into different teams and mixed in with other VBC provider product and VBC Secondary Use teams. Explorys Customer Services were merged in with other VBC services teams. On paper this does make some sense, but it really only makes sense as an optimization of a stable and coordinated organization. Reflecting on the Chilmark comment the prior year on "lack of market vision": a re-org does not vision make, and it made the barriers to effective planning and execution even higher.

The Secondary Use team was now treated pretty much like a stand-alone unit, even though nearly all their clinical data came from the Provider products and customer. The critical relationship Secondary Use and Provider sectors seemed to be lost on far too many people, even within VBC as Phytel didn't have a Secondary Use business, and while Truven did it was based on claims data. If the Provider sector gains customers that was a good thing for Secondary Use, but it also worked in reverse: if the Provider sector lost customers, then Secondary Use decreased. Portfolio planning between Secondary Use and Provider sectors, which was hard enough with IBM and broader Watson Health distractions, now went in the ditch.

Secondary Use communication now came in two flavors: either we couldn't get any communication from the Secondary Use team in terms of where they were going or what they needed, or they would come to us emergency-style saying that a pharmaceutical company would pay $X thousand for some biomarkers processed from clinical notes, and they needed an answer right now. Aside from the obvious issue of the Secondary Use and Provider Offering Management teams not being on the same page, Secondary Use of data is called that for a reason: it is *second*. The Provider sector is supposed to be *first* use. The general principle is that if certain biomarkers should be processed from clinical notes, the Provider sector customers should have access and utility from that data first. That wasn't happening.

To be clear, I don't fault the any of the Secondary Use customers for asking for these data use-cases, nor do I fault any of the Secondary Use staffers for responding to the requests. The issue was a loss of focus on Provider solutions as the foundation of the analytics business. If the providers are successful, then everybody wins. Instead, the new strategy seemed to do as little as possible for the Providers, maximize Secondary Use revenue, and somehow retain data rights.

Separating Services into another organization produced some unintended but still predictable side-effects as there was less emphasis on the operational success of current customers, where Explorys had earned a reputation of being for being responsive over the years, and far more emphasis on finding new billable activities. This would become evident in industry analyst rankings in the not-too-distant future.

Explorys and Epic

It's an exaggeration to say that in healthcare all roads lead to Epic. Perhaps not all, but enough. Explorys was quite familiar with Epic as a data source, but this dynamic was frequently misunderstood and mischaracterized. A 2018 article in STAT stated:

> one of Watson's companies, Explorys, found a way to get behind Epic's firewall and use patient data to fulfill its contractual obligations with its client hospitals.

This is off on several points. Explorys was a part of Watson Health, not Watson. This was a constant source of public confusion, and I had to address whether Watson – especially the talking Watson computer depicted in IBM's TV spots – was automatically getting access to "all the healthcare data" on several occasions. Watson Health and Watson were two different divisions in IBM, but IBM didn't help matters by doing things like branding the business cards for IBM Watson Health employees with a big "IBM Watson" logo on the back.

Most importantly, Explorys did not "hack" or "get behind" Epic's firewall. Bypassing a firewall is a serious allegation that minimally implies disregard for security policy. The above quote is at least half-right in that Epic integration was performed under contract with client hospitals, and that is the important part. Explorys *only* accessed Epic on behalf of its healthcare customers, and in the context of a customer engagement.

During the timeframe Explorys was in business, Epic's electronic health record (EHR) software was typically deployed for a customer in an on-premise environment (i.e., in a data center leased or operated by the healthcare customer), and especially so for the mid/large-sized deployments. Epic's EHR has a few core data components: Chronicles (the operational data store), and Clarity (the data warehousing platform). Chronicles is supported on a database technology called Intersystems Cache. Clarity is supported on Oracle, SQL Server, and Teradata. These technical factoids about Epic were all over the internet and were not secrets.

I had experience with distributed data collection for over five years even before Explorys, and then with Explorys we were able to take data integration to another level. Epic may not have always been happy with this because it presented additional competition to their own analytic products, but that is a separate conversation.

Watson Health Flailing – 2017

Stop The World

In 2017 Explorys experienced three *Stop The World* planning cycles. In **one** year. I had never experienced anything like it in my career. It was excruciating and demoralizing.

Stop The World is a reference to the Java programming language and its garbage collector. Most of the Explorys codebase was written in Java, and Java supports automatic memory garbage collection as opposed to languages such as C and C++ which do not. Automatic garbage collection is generally a very good thing, except when it isn't. In the simplest terms, *minor* garbage collections were where a partial section of the Java Virtual Machine's memory would get cleaned up in the background while your code continued to run. A *full* garbage collection is where everything gets cleaned up and the entire Java Virtual Machine (JVM) is locked – nothing else runs in the process and the world effectively stops. Full collections were an inherent risk of long running Java processes and especially for those with very large memory heap-sizes. Fortunately, there are JVM knobs that could be tweaked and some coding patterns that could implemented to lower the probability of their occurrence.

We had no such knobs to prevent what was headed our way in Watson Health.

Early 2017 we were given a list of sizable efforts to estimate across the portfolio and it would take a week or two with all the engineering leads to figure out what was possible. And this was a top-to-bottom planning exercise because certain things were going to stop happening once this plan went into effect, and then those changes needed to be communicated. With such an effort it's not just the leads that get pulled in, this also requires senior developers to get pulled in to make and confirm estimates. And when those developers get pulled to discussions like that it eats into what they were already committed to do.

But at least we had a direction and the teams were off and running. Until a few months later, when we weren't.

Then it was back to re-planning. And it wasn't a minor touch-up to the plan, some of the major efforts we had been identified as priorities were now on the shelf.

Then we were off and running again. Until a few months later, when we weren't.

Three times in one year. It was utterly insane and the opposite of productivity.

Watson Health was thrashing. Sinking. We could feel it.

Now, Soon, Later

Offering Management started introducing a new paradigm for product road-mapping in 2017 and 2018. Customers would look at a PowerPoint with three columns and were told that features would come *Now*, *Soon*, and *Later*.

This didn't make any sense to us, and the remaining Explorys customers didn't like it much either.

Just trying to define *Now* was ambiguous. Are we talking about *tonight*? This may sound like taking the question too literally, but it's not. Explorys had application releases *weekly*, and sometimes more frequently when hotfixes were required. That cadence was way ahead of what anybody else was doing within Watson Health. The Explorys backend components had even more flexibility and were releasing code to production most days. This week? Next week? End of the month? Is this the kind of *Now* we're talking about?

Even saying "we're working on it *now*" is both too much and not enough information. Is it being researched? Is it understood? Is it being developed? While knowing that development is progressing is nice, what users typically want to know is when something will be *available*.

If defining *Now* was problematic, trying to define *Soon* got even murkier.

And if *Soon* was murky, what the hell did *Later* mean?

As I said, this did not go over well with customers as far as I could tell.

I preferred calendar quarters for anticipated delivery, at least for starters. Calendars are generally understood by most humans who engage in timekeeping and scheduling, and using calendar quarters as a target-range still leaves some room for schedule adjustments until targets could be refined to the month-level. But what do I know, I'm just an engineer.

Operating System Crazy Making

Explorys had been running Red Hat Enterprise Linux (RHEL) for years, and IBM Finance came to us complaining about the multiple hundreds of thousands of dollars of license fees we were paying every year.

After some careful consideration, and because of the excellent work the DevOps team had put in place with automated patching, the DevOps team rolled out CentOS, the open-source version of RHEL, to all the servers. IBM Finance was happy.

We thought we had done a good thing.

But IBM Research didn't like what we had done because while RHEL was an IBM approved operating system CentOS was not. IBM Research wanted us to migrate to Ubuntu. Long story short package management with Ubuntu/Debian is different than RHEL-based package management (apt vs. yum) so "just switching" to Ubuntu was a non-trivial ask, even irrespective of everything else that was going on.

We stayed with CentOS, satisfying one part of IBM but unfortunately leaving another part of IBM displeased. It seemed impossible to do otherwise.

Integration Approaches

My VP of Development flew down to another Watson Health technical offsite in North Carolina. I wasn't on the list which didn't bother me, but he wanted me all the call listening just in case. That was fine.

I was listening to the meeting for a few hours and it was clear it wasn't going well. This meeting was supposed to last for two days. I said it first. "I can fly down there" I messaged.

I wasn't kidding. I really didn't want to go down there, but I'd rather be in the middle of that situation trying to deal with in-person with along my VP of Development than on the phone feeling accountable but ineffective. I got an immediate reply. Sometimes movies will depict a scene where someone has the sudden realization of an immediate travel need and they drive straight to the airport and hop on a plane. That of course is just a storytelling device. That day, it really happened, and I was that person.

I looked at the IBM Travel site and saw that there just happened to be a nonstop in a few hours. I booked it, raced home, threw a change of clothes in my travel bag and then drove right to the airport. I arrived in time for the group's dinner outing.

The next day it got real. It was a continuation of API discussions and integration between Explorys and Phytel, but with way too many cooks in the kitchen. The Watson Health Architecture team, along with the Truven CTO, wanted this built "according to the target architecture," whatever that meant. We needed to use an Enterprise Service Bus (ESB) approach. The ESB phrase was long in the tooth by then, but even taking the idea at face value the devil was always in the details in terms of precisely what anybody actually meant when they said that. Even if we did do that, what bus? Deployed where? Running what software?

Discussions got heated.

What I wanted, as well as one of the senior Phytel staff members, was to use whatever means necessary to get this up and running and fast. Phytel was deployed in a commercial data center in Dallas and Explorys was deployed in a different commercial data center in Cleveland. But provided we had connectivity, the Explorys Services team could use its configurable integration framework and treat Phytel like the hundreds of other data sources Explorys had seen and pull it into Explorys' Data Lake *that afternoon*, and well as schedule for regular updates. It wasn't the fanciest method, but if one is operating in crisis mode that approach can get something working with minimum of new development and then we could iterate from there.

If one is operating in crisis mode, one could make that decision, that is.

I was operating in crisis mode, and so was my VP of Development. We were well aware of the Chilmark review the previous year, and so was Phytel. We were both feeling the heat of shrinking business. The Watson Health Architecture team was not. Neither was Truven's CTO. They were having abstract conversations about a target architecture about a future platform. Which is a great idea in concept if the customers would stick around who knows how many years and wait for it. We could have also started with a basic integration two years earlier, in fact, and shown the market we were serious about bring the products together.

We did wind up being told to build an API-based approach for bidirectional integration with Phytel through 2017. It was a nice development effort, but unfortunately never wound up being utilized by any customers. The effort started two years too late to have an impact.

Blockchain

Blockchain became a much-hyped technology during this time, and IBM could not resist jumping on the bandwagon. In a January 2017 article titled "IBM Watson, FDA Aim to Tackle, Tame Blockchain for Data Exchange" an IBM executive said:

> Blockchain technology has advanced and has matured. At the core, this technology can address various frictions in the health system, such as **meaningful collaboration and coordination** in healthcare that require addressing **privacy concerns, lack of interoperability,** and the **issue of trustworthiness of data**.

And then went on to also say:

> For providers it can provide the **continuity of the health record** and the **longitudinal 360 view of the patient** that the providers need in order to **provide the health services to the patient.**

I have emphasized certain words in the quotations, such as "privacy concerns," "continuity of the health record," and "longitudinal 360 view of the patient" because those phrases mean specific things in healthcare. Those phrases tend to get people's attention and set expectations on capabilities. Yet how blockchain would specifically address those points is never made clear.

One of our customers saw the story and contacted us wondering what those words meant for their organization and their data. They worried, among other things, that their patient's data was going to wind up on an (immutable) IBM blockchain. Complicating matters, I was unable to get anyone in IBM's Blockchain group, who was IBM group behind the article – not Watson Health – to explain the claims in the article and what they were specifically proposing, especially with on-chain and off-chain data. "On-chain" data is data that is actually stored in the blockchain, and "off-chain" data is what is stored anywhere else (e.g., in a relational database). What tended to happen was that, for projects that employed blockchain, to be labeled entirely as "blockchain solutions" even though they were only using blockchain in a very narrow way. I had to start some defensive reading about Hyperledger, a blockchain framework favored by IBM for private blockchain use-cases. I concede private blockchains might actually be useful and entirely appropriate in some cases – it's a big world and there are a lot of problems to solve – but it was yet another distraction.

Once More with Db2

We were asked yet again where we could use Db2, outside of all the SuperMart and Data Warehousing conversations. Explorys used MySQL for internal operations and other metadata. Not big data per se, but very important data just the same.

Given that Explorys customers never saw this database it was an implementation detail in the extreme. Swapping out MySQL for Db2 wasn't crazy in concept for broad IBM technical consistency, and we didn't specifically have a major issue against Db2 itself. IBM created the relational model through Codd's research in the 1960s and had been developing relational data management systems since the 1970s with System R, SQL/DS, and Db2. But given everything else that was happening with the business making this particular technology swap out a priority discussion was madness.

IBM Recruiting

As described earlier Explorys had invested a lot in college recruiting, both for full-time as well as interns and co-ops. We knew how to find talent.

The Spring of 2017 saw an ominous development. Explorys had three openings for software interns and we had gone through our recruiting and interview processes to find three great candidates. We were ready to make offers but then IBM Recruiting stepped in and said that we couldn't make any offers until *they* interviewed the candidates.

One candidate immediately accepted another offer with another company. The candidate's preference was to work with us at IBM Watson Health, but they could tell it was a bad sign that they were being asked to re-interview. I don't blame them. The other two candidates were given a programming test by IBM Recruiting and we were told that they both failed, and we couldn't make them offers. These "test failures" say more about IBM Recruiting that it did about the candidates. IBM Recruiting was telling us we didn't know how to find talent, which we knew was demonstrably false.

We wound up with no interns the Summer of 2017.

The Whiteboards

The obvious question is how and why so many smart people could screw things up so badly within Watson Health. The ability to make bad decisions is easier than you might think, especially at a big company. One important factor is whether a person making a decision has to live the consequences of that decision.

Take for example the Explorys office during the 2016–2018 period at 1111 Superior, which was the first "Designed By IBM" office. Rather than assembling our own desks as in previous Explorys offices, in this new space we now had real grown-up office furniture, which was exciting.

Figure 9.1 Breakout rooms in Explorys IBM office (2016).

But when we moved in August 2016 we saw monitors mounted onto whiteboards in *every* breakout room.

One room would have been a hilarious accident. This was on purpose.

Software engineers like monitors and whiteboards. But this wasn't a Reese's Peanut Butter Cup situation where adding them together made things better.

I don't fault the installers for this. I'm sure when they received the work orders they probably shook their heads in puzzlement, but then thought "that's what the paperwork says" and started making holes. A discreet inquiry was later made as to the design intention, and the alleged response was that the configuration was a "best practice" that "merged digital with the physical." Which is fair, because merging things is what screws and a power drill tend to do. It appeared that the IBM facilities people had neither owned nor leased many dry-erase markers, let alone used them.

But the real question is how many people knew about this idea before it happened and said nothing about it. This illustrates the importance of *Power Distance* in decision-making, a subject innovatively studied at IBM by Geert Hofstede in the late 1960s and early 1970s when researching cross-cultural psychology. IBM not only has a high *Power Distance* which describes the sizable relationship and communication distance from staff to executive levels, but also a high *Power Wannabe Distance* from people who don't like to have their decisions questioned, irrespective of context or actual rank. The *Wannabe* distance isn't something that Hofstede actually described, but it should have been, because it contributes to the inability or unwillingness of people to raise concerns for fear of being labeled an "acquisition troublemaker" and a "whiteboard purist."

Fortunately, this situation had a remedy: our engineering executive finally persuaded facilities to get *another* set of whiteboards ordered and mounted on the opposite walls, this time without monitors installed on them. Problem solved! On top of managing a development organization and all of the other topics mentioned above in this article, obtaining functioning whiteboards also became an executive-level responsibility. It took an executive escalation to resolve this.

Sometimes it is possible to recover from a bad decision. Sometimes not so much.

Sheer Heart Attack – Fall 2017

KLAS Research is another organization that covers the healthcare technology sector and in October 2017 they said of Watson Health:

> IBM Watson Health's population health suite is a combination of several acquired solutions, and many of their current customers came as a result of these acquisitions. This report focuses on the Explorys and Phytel solutions. Explorys' expertise is around data aggregation and analytics. Phytel Atmosphere is known for care management and was the 2015 Best in KLAS winner for population health. Both solutions are now a part of a broader set of solutions that IBM offers under the umbrella of IBM Watson Health. As a result, IBM Watson Health sees broad adoption across all PHM verticals in this report. **Neither the Explorys nor the Phytel platform has received much development since being acquired, so customers are looking forward to seeing a future strategy evolve.**

The panic that review caused within Watson Health cannot be overstated, and it went right to the top. Far worse than a dagger to the chest of the division, it was a spotlight: a million-Watt illumination of Explorys and Phytel bleeding out since being acquired. It was everything we had been warning about for the last 2.5 years, only now it was being said in public, and not by us.

The KLAS review was accurate in terms of the lack of expansion of Explorys' role in clinical and analytic workflows in the healthcare sector. The customer and patient had ceased to be the center of the mission, at least the mission of Watson Health leadership. It was also accurate in terms of Watson Health's confused message on Explorys' role in the product portfolio. Should customers continue to use Explorys? Wait for the next thing? KLAS was confirming what Chilmark had noted back in February 2016: lack of market vision. It was self-sabotage.

The rush of water was coming faster now. We were actively sinking.

Chapter 10

In Spite of Everything

Uphill and against the Wind

It wasn't exactly true, though, that Explorys "didn't receive much development." In spite of everything that had been happening, and somewhat incredibly, Explorys engineering had been able to continue to make significant advancements in:

- *DevOps* – continued to automate with Infrastructure-as a-Service patterns to enable fast deployment and patching and management, and monitoring
- *Integration* – added FHIR support, near-real time data ingestion, and infrastructure for building future APIs
- *Product features* – added support for IBM's UDMH data model in SuperMart, Measure Evidence highlighting, Measure Studio improvements for measure definition and metadata management, measure and registry engine feature additions, therapeutic data set integration from Explore to SuperMart

Explorys also increased its coordination between teams with something that started off as a joke and wound up being a

DOI: 10.4324/9781003491590-10

useful internal shorthand of work status. "Done" meant a ticket is coded and tested, "Done Done" meant the code has been deployed to production, and "Done Done Done" meant the code was turned on for customers in production. As silly as that sounds, it took a lot of discussion to get to that consensus, but we were better for it.

All of this was terrific work, and it was done to either improve the customer experience or to improve operations. Most of these improvements were sponsored and pushed by engineering to completion. I had put slides together in mid-2017 describing the progress since acquisition:

Production Statistics

- CDGH – 50+ Gateways. There were 50 Client Data Gateway for Health devices deployed at customer sites
- SuperMart Provider – 40 Nodes (with 40 nodes hot standby), 42 TB published nightly. This was the multi-tenant Vertica data warehouse that healthcare customers could access for custom reporting
- SuperMart SecondaryUse – 40 Nodes (40 nodes hot standby), 18 TB published weekly, ~93 views for TDS (Therapeutic Datasets), ~65 TB of Sandbox/Static data. This was the de-identified data warehouse that Life Science and Pharma customers could access, as well as other healthcare customers
- Data Lake – 130 Nodes, with 1.3 PB of data. This was the landing zone implemented in 2014
- Kafka Pipeline – 12 nodes
- Data Reservoir – 240 Nodes, with 2.3 PB of data. This was the main processing grid for published data and pipeline jobs
- Explore – 6 VMs. Virtual machines to serve the Explore application stack
- Core Services – 6 VMs

- EPM – 6 VMs. Virtual machines to serve the Explore application stack
- App Grid – 15 VMs
- API Platform – 8 VMs

Explorys data statistics are impressive even a decade later. The amount of generated data (derived records, risk model calculations, etc.) which also included the already ingested and published records was a nightly statistic from the core pipelines. The following description is from mid-2017, down from the high watermark in mid-2016:

- Total Number of Demographic Records – 150 Million+
- Total Number of Published Patient* Records – 80 Billion+
- Total Number of Generated Patient* Records – 124 Billion+
- Nightly Ingest and Published Records – 2.4 Billion+
- Unique Patient Lives In Universe – 56 Million+

Infrastructure Improvements

- Data Center Migration – this referenced a migration within Expedient when the DevOps team consolidated racks into one building
- CDGH – Client Data Gateway for Health, and rebuilt on Docker
- SuperMart – build redundant 40 node clusters
- Data Lake – CDH4 – > IOP. The Data Lake was upgraded from Cloudera's Hadoop distribution to IBM's Hadoop distribution called IOP, and then IBM promptly killed IOP
- Data Reservoir – CDH4 – > CDH5. There was a major upgrade of Cloudera's Hadoop distribution v4 to v5. To say this was an enormous effort is an understatement
- Explore – all app servers rebuilt on OpenStack

- Infrastructure – OpenStack private cloud, Ansible fully automated server deploys, 100% server configurations in Puppet, New real-time monitoring platform, Sensu, Legacy Linux to RHEL, CentOS

API Improvements

- Client Data Gateway for Health – the CDGH was a re-platforming of the Explorys HDG, Revised HL7 Connector
- NRT Processing via Kafka Pipelines – added NRT processing support on the platform
- API Platform – framework for continuous delivery of productized APIs, NRT/ADT admission and discharge API, Patient population analysis API, Patient data FHIR API

Feature Improvements

- SuperMart-Provider – implemented IBM's UDMH data model in SuperMart
- Data Reservoir – implemented a variety of Registry Engine and Measure Engine Improvements
- Explore – PowerSearch v2 code complete (a major revision and enhancement of PowerSearch), operationalized the Therapeutic Dataset to SuperMart Export
- EPM – Measure Evidence Highlighting (this was a big effort), implemented a variety of registry features (more search and filter additions), Measure Studio Improvements

Blue Synergy

("Blue Synergy" referred to supporting other IBM products or solutions)

- Client Data Gateway For Health – re-created the Explorys HDG as a new IBM product called the Client Data Gateway For Health

- Jira/Confluence/BitBucket – configured IBM's Single Signon solution for some of our key development tooling
- Data Lake – CDH4 – > IOP. Per above, we upgraded to IBM's Hadoop distribution IOP only to have IBM immediately kill IOP
- SuperMart-Provider – ran a pilot of IBM's BigSQL engine as a potential replacement of Vertica
- SuperMart-SecondaryUse – ran a pilot of dashDB-Local as a potential replacement of Vertica
- HealthTerm for Standardization – collaborated with other units within Watson Health on using the HealthTerm framework for data standardization
- RWE Secondary Use Feed – published Secondary Use data to Watson Health Cloud to support other non-Explorys Watson Health Real World Evidence efforts
- Watson Health FHIR Server – implemented the Watson Health FHIR Server as a part of the Explorys stack
- Explorys on Watson Health Cloud PoT – tried running some of the Explorys stack on the Watson Health Cloud

All of the above items were from an executive summary from 2017 and were not an exhaustive list. In spite of everything, we never stopped trying to push the products and platforms forward to serve our customers.

Lessons in Customer Data Onboarding

Explorys had dozens of healthcare organizations as customers and had onboarded over 400 data sources for its customers. Customer and data onboarding was an important topic as it was a critical path for business growth. As stated before, the high-level understanding of the customer data onboarding process for years was this:

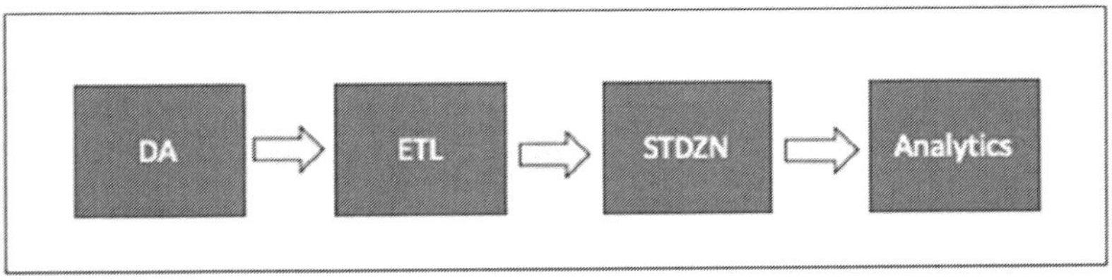

Figure 10.1 Simple understanding of the customer data onboarding process.

Things *generally worked,* and as the saying goes, it was a car that was being built and modified as it was hurtling down the road. It arguably overly relied upon elbow grease and startup heroics, and it was also never entirely clear exactly where time was being spent and why, despite repeated efforts to track it. The Customer Services team put a process flow diagram together to document onboarding activities in detail to get a better handle on the process. Such diagrams are important for understanding complex operations as they have a way of exposing steps that are often taken for granted such as "Bob does XYZ." Evaluating whether Bob is the only person who knows how to do XYZ is a good idea, and likewise, whether

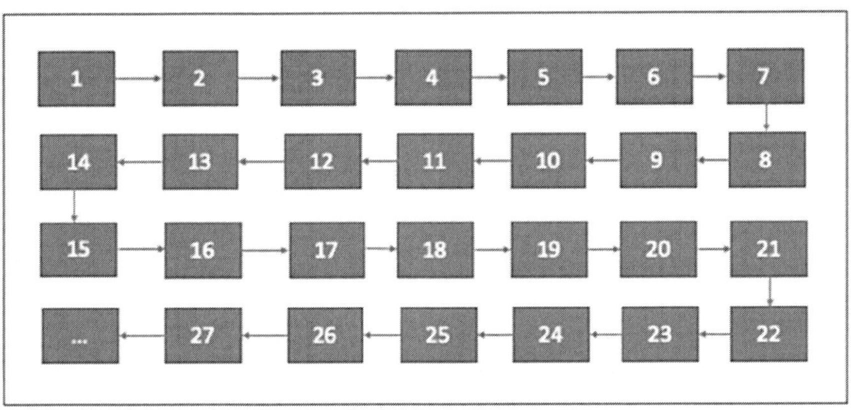

Figure 10.2 A more complex – but entirely linear – customer data onboarding process.

XYZ is a manual step that deserves better tooling is another. The diagram was detailed, with lots of boxes and lines.

It was incrementally useful but it still didn't quite provide the clarity that people were looking for, partly because such diagrams can have an anesthetizing effect at multi-page length. There had to be another dynamic at play.

Identifying Process Concurrency

The engineering team eventually got more deeply involved in this process review, which arguably should have happened earlier but for some executive dynamics which complicated inter-team roadmap planning. I started drawing the process out myself, and then I realized what was missing in the discussions: *the customer onboarding process wasn't linear,* at least not in the way that people drew it. The process really looked like this:

The key was stepping back and internalizing the core value proposition of what Explorys did: for each healthcare customer, Explorys would ingest multiple sources of data, construct

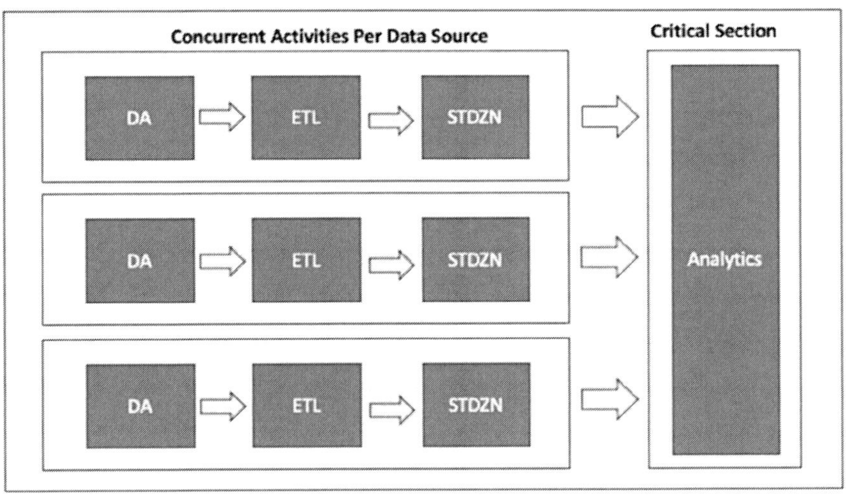

Figure 10.3 Customer data onboarding process, with concurrency.

combined patient records over those multiple sources, calculate a variety of analytics over these records, and have applications to view those results. And not just with one or two data sources, but 5, 10, 15, or more. One customer had over 30 sources. Plus, the sources almost never came in all at once. When a new data source was ingested, there were workstreams that could be performed and tested in isolation from all other data sources, such as data integration (DA) and source-to-target data model transformations (ETL). However, cross data source analytics required a critical section because that is where all the data came together. Onboarding a new source meant that analytic results that had previously been viewed as stable could not only be changed but potentially invalidated.

Somehow, it took years to figure this out.

While I can take credit for drawing the picture, I think just about every staff member involved in the customer onboarding process already knew the punchline but perhaps may not have been able to articulate it. People *knew* that the high-level "DA -> ETL -> STDZN -> Analytics" explanation was sort of directionally correct but also incomplete in a highly problematic way. But the simple understanding of the process hung around longer than it should have because it was easy to write on a whiteboard and put on a PowerPoint, especially for senior staff and executives. It was easier to yell at people to go faster and work harder than to come to terms with a complex process.

The Importance of Data Engineering

Not stated explicitly in the previous pictures was an underlying data engineering pipeline that would:

- *Perform patient matching*:
  - Based on configuration of the patient matching algorithm itself, which was a probabilistic approach based on Fellegi & Sunter (1969)

  - Includes the configured data sources for that customer
- *Construct combined patient record (or "chart")*:
  - Included the standardized attributes per data source, which were subject to fairly frequent changes
  - This step based on the output of patient matching
- *Generate derived record calculations*:
  - Calculating derived records for the combined patient record, such as calculating a BMI (Body Mass Index) if there were height and weight measurements available, as well as performing supplementary data standardization for unit of measure conversions of Observations as needed
  - This step was based on the well as the rest of the combined patient chart, which was in turn based on patient matching
- *Risk model calculations*:
  - Perform dozens of risk model calculations per combined patient
  - This step was based on the generated derived record calculations, as well as the rest of the combined patient chart, which was in turn based on patient matching

There was a lot going on under the hood. All of this data preparation went into the Analytics phase for clinical measure and registry calculations:

Consequently, data issues from new or updated data sources could have a blast radius affecting the entire patient chart and downstream analytics. One small example from Explorys involved height and weight observations which looked suspect in a source from a particular customer but got loaded into production because the data is the data. Think of the Stonehenge scene from the mockumentary *Spinal Tap* where units of measure are confused in a drawing. But when processed at face value a 6-inch or 150-gram person caused

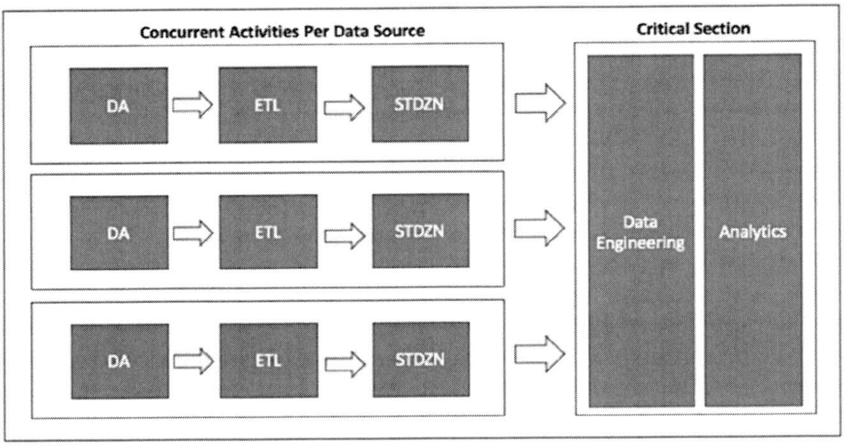

Figure 10.4 Customer data onboarding process, with concurrency and more detail.

the corresponding BMI calculations to go way off scale, as BMI is a ratio of height and weight. BMI values that are off scale in turn caused issues with multiple downstream clinical measures because they included BMI values as criteria. As healthcare data is complex and not always clean, such cases are not unusual.

Managing Operational Data Quality

Separating testing activities from production environments is a long-established best practice. Lower environments typically look like this:

- **DEV** – smaller environments testing all components of a solution (from integration to applications and reporting), but only for a subset of the data, and only periodically refreshed
- **QA** – larger environments testing all components of a solution

So far so good. But managing these environments is an art. In the age of on-premise and statically provisioned infrastructure, having a QA environment that was equivalent to production was a rare luxury, and while Explorys' QA environment was sizable, it was not equal to production. Even in cloud-native solutions, having a full-sized testing environment is something that should never be taken for granted. Similarly, having QA being an up-to-the-minute replica of production (minus the data or analytics subject to testing and validation, of course) is another testing luxury. QA environment data has a tendency to trail by days, weeks, or sometimes months as it isn't just about having the appropriate system capacity; there also need to be automated processes to both rebuild the environments and sync the data. The more manual the processes, the longer the refresh cycles.

Explorys used QA as a pre-production environment to test *code* in terms of functional and performance tests, but not as the standard data route to production. This is not to say that Explorys took a *Damn The Torpedoes* approach in publishing data, though. Quite the opposite, in fact, as many

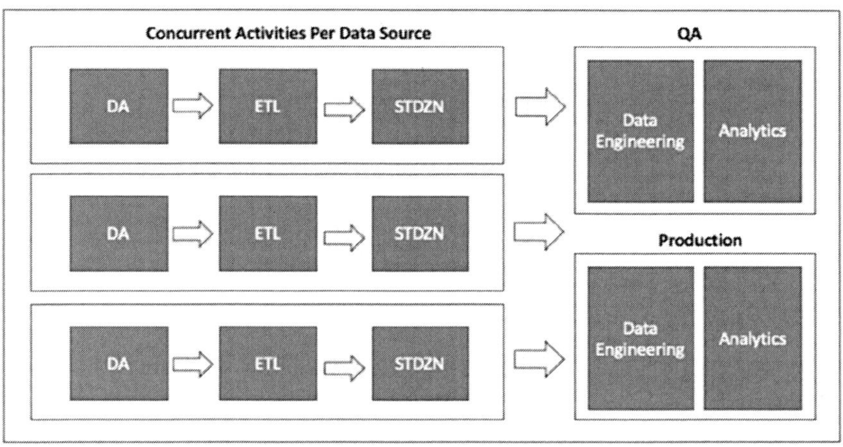

Figure 10.5 Customer data onboarding process, with concurrency and multiple environments.

safeguards were built into the technical stack. First, new data sources could be published to the underlying datastore but not included in the patient chart based on pipeline configurations. Also, there was a rolling retention window of all data engineering pipeline output for each customer, such that in the event of data issues, the active version for a given customer could be set to yesterday instead of today if required. The retention windows meant that we not only had a large amount of published data in the production cluster, but we had a rolling window of multiple copies of that data. Since we were utilizing a distributed architecture, this was an easy pattern to implement, and it was used more than a few times as exotic healthcare data scenarios have a way of showing up at the worst times.

In the End

The process and technology improvements for customer data onboarding represented some great multi-team collaboration. Unfortunately, by the end of 2017, it was clear the customer pipeline had drastically slowed.

Chapter 11

Meanwhile...

Cleveland Clinic Innovations

Envy can do strange things to people, and it must not have been easy for Cleveland Clinic Innovations Director Gary Fingerhut to watch Explorys succeed. Innovation is easy, right? Especially for Cleveland Clinic and its Innovations spinoffs.

Fingerhut started at Cleveland Clinic Innovations in 2010 and became Executive Director in 2013. Fingerhut knew Explorys well, given that Cleveland Clinic Innovations had an Explorys board seat. Fingerhut was fired in 2015 and eventually convicted in 2018 for embezzling $2.7 million dollars through a Cleveland Clinic Innovations company called Interactive Visual Health Records (IVHR). IVHR's mission was to create digital charting software for doctors and was another software startup like Explorys – or was supposed to be. Just sprinkle some code and watch it grow!

IVHR was utilizing a firm called ISTAR that was supposed to be doing software development on its behalf, but ISTAR was actually a shell company set up by IVHR's CTO and Fingerhut. They got away with it for a couple of years. Explorys, despite its warts, was the real deal, and as this book

DOI: 10.4324/9781003491590-11

describes, it took a lot of hard work from a lot of people to make it happen. Cleveland Clinic Innovations would do well to study these lessons on what it takes to foster actual innovation. It's not as easy as it looks.

Fingerhut was sentenced to 30 months in prison.

Theranos

Fame and money can also do strange things to people's judgment.

As described in the book *Bad Blood* by John Carreyrou about Theranos, the multi-billion dollar blood testing fraud founded by Elizabeth Holmes, Rupert Murdoch called Cleveland Clinic CEO Dr Toby Cosgrove for a reference on Theranos in 2015 before he considered investing a massive sum of money – over $100 million – in the company. Theranos already had blood on its hands after the death of its Chief Scientist Ian Gibbons in 2013, but like so many things about Theranos, that wasn't well known at the time. Dr Cosgrove had "nothing but good things to say about Theranos" and Murdoch proceeded with his investment in Theranos. The Cleveland Clinic also announced a partnership with Theranos in March 2015. The joint press-release stated:

> Theranos Inc. and Cleveland Clinic today announced a long-term strategic alliance designed to enhance clinical quality, improve turnaround times, reduce the cost of care, and increase patient satisfaction through Theranos' less invasive, lower cost testing, and a commitment to pursuing the full potential of Theranos technology at Cleveland Clinic and across the broader healthcare system.
>
> Cleveland Clinic's best-in-class pathology team in the Robert J. Tomsich Pathology and Laboratory

Medicine Institute will collaborate with Theranos to provide advanced clinical diagnostic services and, over time, implement Theranos' groundbreaking, CLIA-certified laboratory services within Cleveland Clinic's patient populations.

Theranos offers a full spectrum of laboratory tests, from the most common panels to highly specialized tests, on blood samples as small as a few drops. This eliminates the need for larger needles and numerous vials of blood required for many diagnostic lab tests. Theranos' minimally invasive sample collection will serve patients such as those receiving oncologic, pediatric and other inpatient treatment requiring frequent blood draws. Theranos tests are also priced at 50 percent of Medicare reimbursement rates or less to reduce the overall cost of care.

"Healthcare innovation is essential to making care more accessible, affordable and timely for patients. This relationship could open up new opportunities for both patients and physicians to be part of high-quality, low-cost healthcare," said Toby Cosgrove, M.D., President and CEO of Cleveland Clinic. "We're excited to begin exploring new initiatives that can offer improved care for our patient's healthcare dollar."

In addition, the long-term strategic collaboration between Theranos and Cleveland Clinic includes opportunities to pursue research studies, clinical trials, the development of new tests, and the provision of reference laboratory services through Cleveland Clinic Laboratories. The collaboration may also extend to other Cleveland Clinic hospitals and family health centers.

"Since we launched our first Wellness Center in late 2013, Theranos has been working to make

> actionable information accessible to individuals and their physicians at the time it matters most," said Elizabeth Holmes, Theranos' founder and CEO. "This alliance with a world-renowned health system like Cleveland Clinic furthers our mission, and is another step in our work to bring access to high-quality, affordable lab testing to everyone and help improve the quality and cost of care," added Holmes.
>
> Theranos currently provides its laboratory services through its network of Theranos Wellness Centers, located inside select Walgreens stores across Arizona and in Northern California.

With quotes from both Toby Cosgrove, M.D., President, and CEO, and future felon Elizabeth Holmes within two short paragraphs of each other, I'm sure the Cleveland Clinic would like to forget this ever happened. But while Cleveland Clinic might explain this in hindsight as "just an evaluation" of Theranos' technology, the opening paragraph alone reads like a de facto endorsement. It represented a signal to the rest of the healthcare industry that Theranos was on the level and could be trusted. A safer path would have been to quietly validate the Theranos technology and *then* come out with a big partnership press release, but that was not the path taken. This is just before Carreyrou's first *Wall Street Journal* article was published on October 15, 2015, which initiated Theranos' implosion and subsequent criminal investigation. But the decline didn't take effect immediately, and Theranos fought all the way down. Incredible as it may seem, Elizabeth Holmes gave the keynote at the Cleveland Clinic Medical Innovation Summit later in October 2015, held in Cleveland, and not too far from Explorys. Talk about a brush with infamy.

Cleveland Clinic partnered with Theranos for the same reasons that Theranos' early customers Safeway and Walgreens did, as everybody would appreciate a less painful, cheaper, and invasive way to perform blood tests, as long as that alternative isn't fraudulent. But there were other influences likely lurking below the surface, such as a Fear of Missing Out (FOMO), as Cleveland Clinic no doubt worried about a competitor getting access to the technology first or even getting locked out. FOMO was a major factor with Walgreens regarding their arch-rival, CVS. Another potential influence is a desire for fame-association, which Theranos and Elizabeth Holmes certainly were at the time, as Holmes was featured on the cover of *Fortune* magazine in 2014 doing a Steve Jobs impression, among many other glowing headlines and reviews from the time. Both Safeway and Walgreens were out of their clinical depth as retail merchants when dealing with Theranos, but Cleveland Clinic was different. One would think it would have smelled something fishy in the Theranos claims, as Cleveland Clinic was not only a healthcare organization but also *ran its own laboratories*. Although Cleveland Clinic wasn't building their own machines and utilized third-party testing services from LabCorp and Quest for tests not performed in-house, they had to have known more about lab tests than Theranos ever did. Given that the Safeway and Walgreens projects with Theranos were in big trouble at the time of Murdoch's call to Dr Cosgrove, Cleveland Clinic's due diligence on the partnership hopefully would have raised a few questions, especially by early 2015. Yet the reference call yielded nothing but good things to say.

Safeway and Walgreens customers were put at risk due to Theranos' inaccurate lab tests, but fortunately the same did not happen to Cleveland Clinic patients because of Carreyrou's reporting. We all owe a debt to the Theranos insiders who put their careers at risk to speak out, and it is not an exaggeration to say that Theranos did everything in its power to destroy them (see Tyler Schultz and Erika Cheung's experiences with Theranos' private investigators and endless legal threats). As bad as Theranos was, had the fraud persisted further the

Figure 11.1 Tomsich Pathology Laboratories – Cleveland Clinic Main Campus. Unlike Safeway and Walgreens, Cleveland Clinic was not only a leader in healthcare but had experience operating clinical labs.

impact to patients would have been even worse. It is another example of the need to look closer at innovation stories that, on the surface, may sound overly simplistic and too good to be true.

Theranos CEO Elizabeth Holmes and COO Sunny Balwani were found guilty on multiple counts of fraud and sentenced to 11-year and 12-year terms in prison, respectively.

UnifyProject

McHale and Lougheed left Explorys/IBM Watson Health after their two-year retention bonuses were paid out in the Spring of 2017. As a disclaimer, I had a retention bonus as well, but I'm quite certain our amounts weren't nearly the same.

Amazon's Second HQ solicitation in 2017 was both genius and utterly cynical. Amazon had no doubt started with a short list of target cities, but making an open bid process had the makings of a lottery stampede. Cleveland didn't have a realistic chance of becoming the second headquarters, but I don't fault any of the city leaders for at least submitting *something* and going through the process. Unfortunately, it was also a great opportunity for hucksters and snake oil.

Per a *Cleveland Scene* article that came out July 11, 2018, "An Essay on the Failed Amazon Bid and the Defective Philosophy Undermining Cleveland's Progress," a nebulous and fledgling effort called "UnifyProject" was at the center of the bid, McHale and Lougheed's latest creation. This small section of the article is but a sample of just how outrageous the bid was:

> The Unify Project, styled throughout the bid as a single word, appeared on the package's very first page of text after the table of contents. It was extolled as one of the top five regional selling points by Cleveland mayor Frank Jackson and county executive Armond Budish.
>
> "Only in Cleveland," they wrote, "the UnifyProject is leveraging the power of big data to create a sustainable investment system that will define health and drive solutions to poverty."
>
> "Poverty is unacceptable, unnecessary and unsustainable," the bid declaimed, a statement belied by the region's policy prerogatives of the past half-century. "The goal of the UnifyProject is to shift from a charity to an investment model and build an inclusive economy that empowers all to live in prosperity. The project focuses on using big data to drive efficiency in redefining health, optimize the use of resources and reshape the medical and health care world to invest in and ensure sustainable, scalable solutions."

Later in the article it was described that UnifyProject was going to address poverty with blockchain technology, which was the Next Hot Technology at the time. And most critically, McHale and Lougheed had declared UnifyProject one of the top five regional assets, even before doing anything.

Claiming to solve poverty with blockchain is bad enough. Claiming to be one of the top five regional assets without doing anything somehow manages to be worse. Cleveland is a classic rust-belt city, but it still has assets: healthcare organizations like Cleveland Clinic and University Hospitals, NASA Glenn Research Center, educational institutions like Case Western Reserve University and Cleveland State University, world-class museums such as the Cleveland Museum of Art, Cleveland Museum of Natural History, and the Rock and Roll Hall of Fame, institutions such as the Cleveland Orchestra and Playhouse Square, and so on. Lake Erie is nice, especially for those who like to drink water. Sports teams like the Cavs, Guardians, and Browns are regional assets too. Sweet Jesus, even the Browns.

UnifyProject had the solution to the vexing problem of systemic poverty, so it claimed, and was a top regional asset. With blockchain.

The reporter's exasperated reaction: "Quoth the raven, 'What the fuck?'"

Indeed.

This wasn't just saying the quiet part out loud; McHale and Lougheed were yelling it. Screaming it, in fact. Both had so thoroughly internalized the Explorys creation story of doing it all themselves that they believed they could do anything, just by saying so.

It might not be a surprise to learn that UnifyProject did not, in fact, end up doing anything. There were several *Cleveland Scene* follow-up articles to that fact. UnifyProject later changed its name to "UnifyLabs" and tried to embed itself within the United Way, which created additional controversies.

This *Cleveland Scene* headline from July 2022 says it all:

> More Fake, Dumb, High-Tech Nonprofits on Horizon as Sharon Sobol Jordan Takes Reins from Augie Napoli at United Way: Among other things: Unify Labs, formerly the Unify Project, is now Unify Jobs.

Unify Jobs later became something else.

Fame and money can do strange things to people.

The Wrap-Up Conversation

The last conversation I had with McHale at Explorys was just before he left in the Spring of 2017. I had multiple conversations with McHale, Dr Jain, and Lougheed over the years about the Explorys creation story, and that it wasn't giving credit to the engineering and product development that actually happened. Dr Jain started full-time at Explorys in 2011, almost two years after the formation, and I had been there since the pre-founding skunkworks – but Dr Jain was a *founder*, and I wasn't. I was okay with being one of four. But I was *not* okay being zero of three. I had heard a variety of excuses from each of them over the years, ranging from claiming that they had no idea what I was talking about to claiming that they had no idea what I was talking about and I was over-reacting.

But this time McHale finally said the quiet part out loud.

> "Because you didn't negotiate being a founder in your offer letter."

Mind you this was 2017 and we had been having this conversation periodically at least since late 2011, shortly after Dr Jain joined, and now he was referring back to when Explorys formed in late Summer of 2009. I was there for that formation, and before. It was an empty explanation for someone who claimed to be a "Servant Leader." While it wasn't materially different from all his other excuses, this somehow explained everything. I wasn't a part of the story he wanted to tell. It didn't matter what I actually did for Explorys. I was a parking spot. Something to be negotiated.

"and the three men brought Explorys to life."

Chapter 12

The End of Watson Health

Implosion

There were significant layoffs in Watson Health in May 2018, and the headlines for the rest of the year and next were terrible. There was immense irony in IBM going from a company of innovation and lifetime employment to having a core competency in firing people.

> IBM's problems with Watson Health run deeper than recent layoffs, former employees say.
>
> **STAT – June 2018**

> Layoffs at Watson Health Reveal IBM's Problem With AI.
>
> **IEEE Spectrum – June 20, 2018**

> Head of IBM Watson Health leaving post after company stumbles, growing criticism.
>
> **STAT – October 2018**

DOI: 10.4324/9781003491590-12

The details of the articles didn't get any better.

From *IEEE Spectrum* (2018):

- "We pivoted so many times."
- "While the engineers tried to follow the shifting directions from above, Phytel didn't deliver anything new to the market."
- "they really thought IBM would take it to the next level—not destroy it within three years."

While the above comments were from the Phytel employees, they were basically the same as the Explorys experiences described in this book.

From STAT (2018):

- *"There was a lot of internal friction," one of the former employees told STAT. "There were two products that did exactly the same thing, that were being sold by two different parts of the company, that had two different development roadmaps."*
- *"Watson Health's various business units were too focused on their own growth, which discouraged collaboration. Coupled with the company's failure to combine their newly acquired companies and align their cultures and operations, IBM was laden with duplicative products and services in a way that was all but cost efficient."*

These comments are also largely true, but I would alter one of the phrases from "focused on their own growth" to "focused on their own **survival**." It should be clear from this book that there was little that IBM Watson Health did to effectively promote the *growth* of acquisition business cases. Growth in the acquisitions, where possible, was the result of sheer force of will in the face of massive internal headwinds. There was some great work achieved despite a cyclone of distractions, and there were a lot of people who worked tirelessly to support Explorys, especially our Integration Executive and VP of Development.

Just a few months after the IBM acquisition in the Summer of 2015, another senior Explorys engineer and I were privately predicting that we would have three years to make Watson Health work, at best, based on the laws of country music songs about relationships. We saw Explorys progressing through the following phases in one-year increments:

- *The Yelling* –The volume of customer complaining, which was already loud due to the confusion in Offering Management, would increase from customers who wanted to know about product roadmaps and proposed projects
- *The Silence* – Then the volume of complaining would drop. It would *seem* like things were getting better on the customer front, but what was actually happening is that RFPs were being sent out for our replacement
- *The Leaving* – Then, breaking the silence, contract terminations would start dropping like bombs. The terminations would seem like a surprise to those not paying attention, but they really weren't

Unfortunately, that is precisely what happened.

I was listening to a call with my VP of Development around April 2018 when one of Explorys' last big customers was threatening to leave, and that was the first I heard Watson Health General Manager Deborah DiSanzo express any concern about saving acquisition customers. She was practically in a panic, which I did strangely appreciate. But it was a recognition of danger far too late. Three years too late.

Then the layoffs happened the following month and blew any remaining air out of the business, and people started to look for the exits.

When my VP of Development left in the Summer of 2018, a Watson Health Cloud executive told him "you were a great competitor."

The last word lingered.

"Competitor."

Again, the quiet part out loud. He was not referring to market competition.

"Competitor?? We were supposed to be on the same team!" was my VP of Development's reply.

By October 2018, DiSanzo was out as the head of Watson Health, but the damage had been done. Concurrently, KLAS dropped its coverage of Explorys. Explorys was functionally dead in the eyes of the market.

I grant that Watson Health was a worthy idea, and even an admirable one. But as undertaken, there were too many conflicting priorities, and it was too much to manage at once, especially with an expectation of not just hockey-stick revenue growth but profitability as well – two distinct attributes that take time to manage and optimize. There was also an underlying condescension toward the acquisition companies exemplified by that *competitor* comment. The acquisitions, imperfect as they were, at least had functioning products and customer services, and those solutions could be extended and expanded. IBM thought it could buy healthcare customers and access to the data, and then those customers would just keep paying IBM for years on end without any improvements to their existing solutions, simply because they were *IBM*. That shouldn't make any sense to anyone with product development experience. If you are an IBM executive who only speaks to other IBM executives, however, it somehow did.

UrbanCode

As incredible as this may seem, Explorys wasn't IBM's first software acquisition in Cleveland. IBM acquired a company called UrbanCode which produced Continuous Integration/ Continuous Deployment (CI/CD) software in 2013, with one of its core products being AnthillPro, build management software based on the Ant build framework. Explorys didn't work that closely with UrbanCode, but we knew each other socially as Cleveland is a big small-town. We would occasionally compare notes. One of the perspectives that somebody from UrbanCode shared with me was that within IBM there was the *outside* world and then there was the *inside* world – and those two things had nothing to do with each other. Promotions and advancement in IBM are based on the latter, not the former. Every now and again there was a reconciliation between those two worlds, and the trick was to not be around when that happened because it usually wasn't pleasant.

That sounded familiar.

That kind of inside-outside dynamic could happen in any large organization, IBM just had its own special brand. IBM later sold off UrbanCode to HCL in about 2018.

One Final Move

Fifth Office

The fifth office (August 2018) was a new IBM building at E. 105th and Cedar next to the Cleveland Clinic Main Campus. Explorys was back in Cleveland's University Circle. It turned out to be a really nice office. The office had a break room, quality conference rooms, and a training room for either internal or customer presentations. It had even had a ping-pong table in an enclosed room to keep the balls and noise contained, which was awesome. Even the whiteboards worked. This idea for this office had been in the works for years as a permanent home for Explorys back across from the Cleveland Clinic. Unfortunately, by the time construction finished and we

Figure 12.1 IBM Cleveland office in 2022 sitting empty.

moved in the business had caved. I'm sure that IBM Finance tried to kill this project in the first half of 2018 but somehow couldn't, and the construction still ran to completion by inertia and fumes, probably aided by tax abatements and promises of future employment numbers that would never materialize.

It was a weird move-in. Normally an office move marks a new era of growth. This move was met with sighs of "let's see how long this lasts." It's a nice building though.

When Covid-19 hit in March 2020 the office, already sparsely utilized, became an empty shell.

Departure

I had tried everything in my power to keep the business afloat and failed. As much as I loved working with the team, I had to leave for my own sanity in January 2019, and I got a clap out from the remaining engineers. I had done it for others, and

Figure 12.2 I once got this close to Ginni Rometty at a corporate event for IBM Distinguished Engineers. But by April 2018, when this picture was taken, Watson Health was too far gone.

now it was my turn. The pattern was simple – as the departing colleague approached the door for their final exit, one person from the remaining group, from the comfort of their desk, would start a slow and soft clap, which would be joined by another, then another, and then gradually form into modest applause. Not so much an applause of celebration, but one of recognition. The clap was acknowledged by the departing with a quick wave.

I must admit I got misty-eyed.

Thank you. It meant a lot.

The Art of Not Learning

Ginni Rometty, IBM CEO, appeared on the Lex Fridman podcast in March 2023 for a long-form interview. Rometty was

IBM CEO from 2012 to 2020, just after the Jeopardy project in 2011. Rometty was CEO for the creation of the Watson Health division in 2015 and most of its existence. Although Rometty was on the podcast to promote her book, the topic of Watson and Watson Health came up later in the conversation.

I agree with Rometty when she said – and I am paraphrasing a little – "Watson helped put AI on the map." AI has been researched for decades, but IBM certainly put it back on the map with a proof point. IBM's Jeopardy effort in 2011 was both a technical and marketing coup. But when Rometty refers to "Watson," she tends to refer to the Jeopardy project as a whole, and this is an example of where IBM's troubles started with expectation management. What Rometty didn't articulate was that the Jeopardy effort – as fascinating as it was, and it *really* was – was a Jeopardy-playing machine. Especially in the afterglow of Jeopardy's success, IBM saw *every* problem as a Jeopardy board, the obvious issue being that few things looked exactly like Jeopardy except *Jeopardy*. It was the hammer-and-nail analogy come to life.

I also agree with Rometty when she said "AI needs to be treated like an ingredient." AI is best used as a component that could be utilized within larger solutions. But that certainly wasn't how IBM was treating Watson during the Watson Health era, and it certainly wasn't the Explorys experience with Watson. Watson was a very difficult ingredient to access, and as acquisitions, we were not encouraged to use it – we were expected to re-write our entire solutions.

I take issue, though, with her comment "it's right or wrong what took us down the path of healthcare first with AI" as if going into healthcare was a roll of the dice between the financial sector, retail, or riverboat casinos. Or healthcare. Rometty seems to have forgotten about her own 2015 comments about healthcare being IBM's *Moonshot*, and that Watson Health was set up as entirely new IBM division in 2015. New divisions in IBM are significant and don't happen that often. There were highly publicized project blow-ups, such as the Watson for Oncology deployment at MD Anderson, one of the top cancer centers in the country. Watson and Watson Health engaged in significant public marketing with TV ads featuring a Cleveland Clinic doctor having a conversation with a talking Watson. The division ended up losing billions of dollars and destroying multiple acquisitions in the process. All of this occurred during Rometty's tenure as CEO. To hear "it's right or wrong" as the executive summary on why IBM got into healthcare was profoundly disappointing.

Rometty's additional commentary on the challenges of Watson implementations were CEO-Smooth but underwhelming and insight-free. When people say, as Rometty did, "the challenges aren't the technology" – it is nearly always the case that the speaker doesn't understand the technology in question. There are *always* technical challenges, especially in healthcare. Rometty mentioned the importance of "human change management," which is fair, but without any follow-up with examples to indicate any specific understanding. And when she said "don't just put it (i.e., AI) on something – think about the process" – that is also fair, but what Rometty seemed to be implying was that the Luddites at MD Anderson, for example, were too set in their ways to recognize Watson's AI intrinsic awesomeness, and *that* was why Watson for Oncology failed.

I would have hoped that Rometty would have said something like this with respect to the Watson Health initiative:

1) We took a big swing at healthcare – in fact, I called it a Moonshot
2) We underestimated the complexity of healthcare in many ways
3) We overpromised in too many places
4) It didn't turn out like we wanted

I don't think that is too much to ask, but I didn't hear anything like that. Rometty's attitude is not unique, though. I saw the same thing across IBM and Watson Health leadership.

With all that time and money spent on Watson Health, IBM appears to have learned nothing. Explorys and the other collateral damage from Watson Health were just so much Armonk roadkill, quickly glanced at from the back of a limousine and then forgotten, if noticed at all.

The What-Ifs

If replayed 100 times, I think that Explorys would have been destroyed nearly every time within IBM Watson Health. Some outcomes might have been slightly less painful, some possibly even worse. Watson Health was just too chaotic and there were too many competing priorities, and on top of that becoming IBM required undoing much of what made Explorys successful in the first place. I do think that a few multiverses may exist where Explorys could have survived within IBM but would have required decisions and compromises that most IBM executives would be loath to make. Compounding the irony is that many of the companies that Explorys was competing against in 2015 are still around a decade later.

Also, reconciling what actually made Explorys successful versus its creation myth would have enabled a more constructive and productive leadership environment within Explorys, and would have improved the chances of its long-term success. That disconnect was not IBM's fault. That responsibility lay squarely with Explorys.

Both were unlikely outcomes. But were not impossible.

IBM aside, Explorys would have had a much better chance of surviving if had been acquired by a company with less complicated and conflicted portfolio. That was a real

Figure 12.3 Explorys Graphic Corporate History by Braun Ink (2015).

possibility given the due diligence in late 2014 and early 2015, but that is water over the dam now.

Had any of those things happened, Cleveland might have had a fighting chance as the healthcare data capital of the world, as depicted in the 2015 Braun Ink cartoon.

One Final Swipe

Although I left IBM in January 2019, I still had one more interaction in store.

My appointment to IBM Distinguished Engineer (DE) in 2016 meant that I was a D-band in the IBM job-grade hierarchy, an IBM executive. The D-band promotion typically comes with a relatively small increase in salary but with an executive bonus plan. The bonus algorithm was described as being one-third about the DE's performance for the year, one-third for the business unit results, and one-third for IBM results as a whole. If one worked a percentage of a year, one was supposed to be "eligible" for the same proportion of that year's plan. Bonuses are paid out in March of the following year.

I was at IBM all through 2018, from January 1st to December 31st. That was a bad year for Watson Health for sure, but IBM still made some money. When the 2018 bonuses were paid out in March 2019, mine was *nothing*. Zero dollars and zero cents.

Ouch!

To be certain, my expectations were small. But *something*, however small, still seemed like a reasonable expectation. I was an IBM executive, and IBM still made money in 2018, after all. Maybe a couple of hundred IBM executive bucks for overall corporate performance. I would have even been happy with a Dick's Sporting Goods gift certificate and a ham sandwich as a token *thank you for trying because you have been warning us for years about what eventually happened.* The zero-bonus message was crystal clear and unambiguous: monitors belong on whiteboards, and don't you forget it.

What can you say? I tried.

Merative

IBM finally sold off the remains of Watson Health in late 2022 to a private equity firm which was rebranded as Merative. There were even more layoffs after that, and then any remaining Explorys solutions that were running were shut down and the servers in the Cleveland data center de-commissioned. It was astonishing that the Explorys solutions were still running at that point, considering that there was almost nobody left from the product teams. Phytel, which was also mortally wounded during Watson Health, was shut down by Merative in 2023. Even Curam didn't escape damage as Merative let

Figure 12.4 Site of the Old Cleveland Playhouse (2023). I was standing a little bit to the right of this traffic circle for the 2016 picture earlier in this book.

over 250 employees go in 2023 in the search for more private equity profits. To quote an affected Curam employee from a news story of the layoffs: "It's not that they're not making money, it's that they're not making enough money."

In 2023 the Cleveland Clinic demolished the Old Cleveland Playhouse, where Explorys was operating from 2012 to 2016, and where it was when acquired by IBM. This wasn't entirely unexpected as Cleveland Clinic had bought the property back in 2009 and there wasn't much in the way of maintenance of the facility, a concern that existed when the Cleveland Playhouse theater company was operating there and before they moved downtown to Cleveland's Playhouse Square district. The demolition, however, was strangely fitting given Explorys' demise. Perhaps the next best legacy for Explorys might be to increase parking capacity for Cleveland Clinic's Main Campus. That would at least be something.

Appendix

References

Preface

- IBM Annual Report 2015
  - https://www.ibm.com/annualreport/2015/assets/img/2016/02/IBM-Annual-Report-2015.pdf
- *The New York Times* on Watson Health 2015
  - https://archive.nytimes.com/bits.blogs.nytimes.com/2015/04/13/ibm-creates-watson-health-to-analyze-medical-data/
- *Forbes* on Watson Health 2015
  - https://www.forbes.com/sites/benkepes/2015/04/16/more-watson-goodness-ibm-announces-health-focused-vertical/
- MarketWatch on IBM 2015
  - https://www.marketwatch.com/story/ibm-reports-another-revenue-decline-2015-04-20-164851813
- *IEEE Spectrum*
  - https://spectrum.ieee.org/how-ibm-watson-overpromised-and-underdelivered-on-ai-health-care
  - https://spectrum.ieee.org/layoffs-at-watson-health-reveal-ibms-problem-with-ai

- STAT News
  - https://www.statnews.com/2018/07/25/ibm-watson-recommended-unsafe-incorrect-treatments/
- *Financial Times* (2021)
  - https://www.ft.com/content/ded67317-682d-4cd9-8e41-fc72646dee12

Innovation

- *Code Breakers,* Walter Isaacson
- "The Real Creators of COBOL"
  - https://ieeexplore.ieee.org/stampPDF/getPDF.jsp?tp=&arnumber=841602&ref=

Explorys Public Stories

- Explorys/Cleveland Plain Dealer
  - https://www.cleveland.com/business/2013/02/big_data_is_starting_to_bring.html
  - https://www.cleveland.com/business/2015/01/big_data_pioneer_explorys_plan.html
  - https://www.cleveland.com/business/2016/08/ibm_eyes_new_office_building_o.html
- *The Cleveland Clinic Way,* Toby Cosgrove MD.

Scaling a Startup

- Explorys/Med City News
  - https://medcitynews.com/2010/08/explorys-raises-2-55m-to-take-healthcare-data-analysis-next-step/
  - https://medcitynews.com/2011/05/health-data-firm-explorys-raises-11-5m-series-c-investment-round/

- History of Explorys
  - https://themeildeal.blogspot.com/2021/01/the-actual-history-of-explorys-part-1.html
  - https://themeildeal.blogspot.com/2021/02/the-actual-history-of-explorys-part-2.html
- Board Games
  - https://ecommons.udayton.edu/news_rls/8918/

Watson Health

- Moonshots
  - https://www.geneticsandsociety.org/article/ibm-ceo-watson-health-our-moonshot-healthcare
  - https://www.youtube.com/watch?v=46MYhalt7EU
  - https://www.ibm.com/policy/ibm-welcomes-u-s-moon-shot-initiative-wipe-cancer/
- Becoming a Distinguished Engineer
  - https://www.clevescene.com/news/night-at-the-museum-for-clevelands-robust-big-data-community-4958936
  - https://www.meetup.com/cleveland-hadoop/events/228560668/
- Explorys and Epic
  - https://www.politico.com/tipsheets/morning-ehealth/2017/08/02/cancer-moonshot-head-recounts-exchange-with-epics-faulkner-221658
  - https://www.fiercehealthcare.com/ehr/editor-s-corner-why-biden-faulkner-exchange-over-ehr-access-touched-a-nerve
  - https://www.fiercehealthcare.com/tech/epic-ceo-judy-faulkner-says-onc-data-blocking-rule-undermines-privacy-and-removes-intellectual

  - https://www.statnews.com/2020/01/27/epic-block-proposed-data-rule/
  - https://www.cnbc.com/2020/01/22/epic-ceo-sends-letter-urging-hospitals-to-oppose-hhs-data-sharing-rule.html
  - https://www.healthit.gov/topic/information-blocking
- Decline
  - https://www.healthcaredive.com/news/ibm-watson-fda-aim-to-tackle-tame-blockchain-for-data-exchange/433833/

Meanwhile

- Cleveland Clinic Innovations
  - https://www.justice.gov/usao-ndoh/pr/solon-man-sentenced-30-months-prison-his-role-conspiracy-defraud-cleveland-clinic-out
- Theranos and Cleveland Clinic
  - https://www.businesswire.com/news/home/20150309005903/en/Theranos-and-Cleveland-Clinic-Announce-Strategic-Alliance-to-Improve-Patient-Care-through-Innovation-in-Laboratory-Testing
  - https://www.theverge.com/2016/2/2/10899162/theranos-cleveland-clinic-dodge-validate-inventions-study
  - https://www.biospace.com/cleveland-clinic-release-b-elizabeth-holmes-b-to-deliver-keynote-address-at-b-2015-medical-innovation-summit-b
  - *Bad Blood,* John Carreyrou
- UnifyProject
  - https://www.clevescene.com/news/an-essay-on-the-failed-amazon-bid-and-the-defective-philosophy-undermining-clevelands-progress-20653840
  - https://www.clevescene.com/news/unify-project-is-now-unify-labs-new-partnership-with-united-way-raises-questions-eyebrows-31470592

- https://www.clevescene.com/news/more-fake-dumb-high-tech-nonprofits-on-horizon-as-sharon-sobol-jordan-takes-reins-from-augie-napoli-at-united-way-39212599

- The Wrap Up Conversation
  - https://my.clevelandclinic.org/about/overview/leadership/board-of-trustees

The End of Watson Health

- Watson Health Implosion
  - Association for Computing Machinery (ACM) – "What Happened To Watson Health?"
    - https://cacm.acm.org/blogs/blog-cacm/252055-what-happened-to-watson-health/fulltext
  - *IEEE Spectrum* – "How IBM Watson Overpromised and Underdelivered on AI Healthcare"
    - https://spectrum.ieee.org/biomedical/diagnostics/how-ibm-watson-overpromised-and-underdelivered-on-ai-health-care
  - *IEEE Spectrum* – "Layoffs at Watson Health Reveal IBM's Problem With AI"
    - https://spectrum.ieee.org/the-human-os/artificial-intelligence/medical-ai/layoffs-at-watson-health-reveal-ibms-problem-with-ai
  - STAT News – "IBM's problems with Watson Health run deeper that recent layoffs, former employees say"
    - https://www.statnews.com/2018/06/11/ibm-watson-health-problems-layoffs/
  - INSEAD – "Challenges in Commercial Deployment of AI: Insights from The Rise and Fall of IBM Watson's AI Medical System"
    - https://publishing.insead.edu/case/challenges-commercial-deployment-ai-insights-rise-and-fall-ibm-watsons-ai-medical-system

- Curam Layoffs
  - https://www.thejournal.ie/merative-workers-layoffs-6187019-Oct2023/
- The Art Of Not Learning
  - Lex Fridman Podcast (with Ginni Rometty)
    - https://www.youtube.com/watch?v=XiCxj-bXu5M

Publications from the Author

- https://www.linkedin.com/pulse/publications-doug-meil/
- A few articles relevant to themes in this book:
- "What Happened to Watson Health?"
  - https://cacm.acm.org/blogs/blog-cacm/252055-what-happened-to-watson-health/fulltext
- "Inorganic Growth in Tech"
  - https://cacm.acm.org/blogcacm/inorganic-growth-in-tech-getting-shredded-with-acquisitions/
- "Design Orientation and Optimization"
  - https://cacm.acm.org/blogcacm/design-orientation-and-optimization/
- "The Art of Speedy Systems Conversions"
  - https://cacm.acm.org/blogcacm/the-art-of-speedy-systems-conversions/
- "The Art of Design Regret"
  - https://cacm.acm.org/blogcacm/software-learning-the-art-of-design-regret/
- "Software Quotes and Counter Quotes"
  - https://cacm.acm.org/blogcacm/software-quotes-and-counter-quotes/
- "Enterprise Metrics and Optimization"
  - https://cacm.acm.org/blogcacm/enterprise-metrics-and-optimization/
- "The Hadoop Ecosystem's Continued Impact"
  - https://cacm.acm.org/blogcacm/the-hadoop-ecosystems-continued-impact/

- "Blockchain for What, Exactly?"
  - https://cacm.acm.org/blogcacm/blockchain-for-what-exactly/

IBM Acquisition Attestation of Cleveland Clinic Intellectual Property

"Jeter" was IBM's codename for the acquisition of Explorys. Intellectual property of all kinds was an explicit point of discussion during acquisition due diligence, and specifically Cleveland Clinic Innovations intellectual property as it related to Explorys (effectively, one of the major themes of this book). None of the information I was relaying was new at the time within Explorys. This email was acknowledged but the response is not included.

From: Doug Meil

Sent: Wednesday, April 08, 2015 10:44 PM

To: Stephen McHale

Subject: [jeter] CCF & Explore IP info

Hey Steve,

Since this came up in the IP discussion, if you need any sound-bites about CCF eResearch influence on Explore. As I also stressed Measure, Registry & SuperMart had nothing to do with eResearch and are 100% Explorys.

1. eResearch was SQLServer & .Net. We don't use any of that.
2. eResearch was using <u>uncompressed</u> bitsets in SQLServer.

We've used compressed bitsets since the beginning, that suggestion came from Todd Lipcon (Cloudera). He suggested

WAH but we later wound up using ConciseSet, and just recently switched to RoaringBitset. eResearch had a patient-orientation the bitset, but we do it concept-oriented.

3. Explore has PowerSearch (huge feature that eResearch didn't have).
4. Explore has Browse The Crowd (another huge feature that eResearch didn't have).
5. Explore has type-ahead term search.
6. Explore supports SNOMED, RxNorm, LOINC – and is backed by the data mapping of the platform, etc. eResearch was aimed at CCF data only.
7. Explore has a way more sophisticated mechanism for creating FastSearches (e.g., ors/ands).

There's more but that's the general idea. Not trying to dump on eResearch, but I said it now represented about 1% of the Explore conceptually.

Doug Meil

Chief Software Architect, Explorys

doug.meil@explorysmedical.com

Population Explorer – Browse The Crowd

Of all the meeting minutes and design documents I wrote up from the early years of Explorys this one stands out as a favorite. I certainly don't claim to be a user interface specialist, but this was my mockup for what would become Population Explorer's "Browse The Crowd." Browse The Crowd was an essential and popular part of live demos of the application both pre- and post-acquisition. The example concepts in the mockup already show how closely we were studying

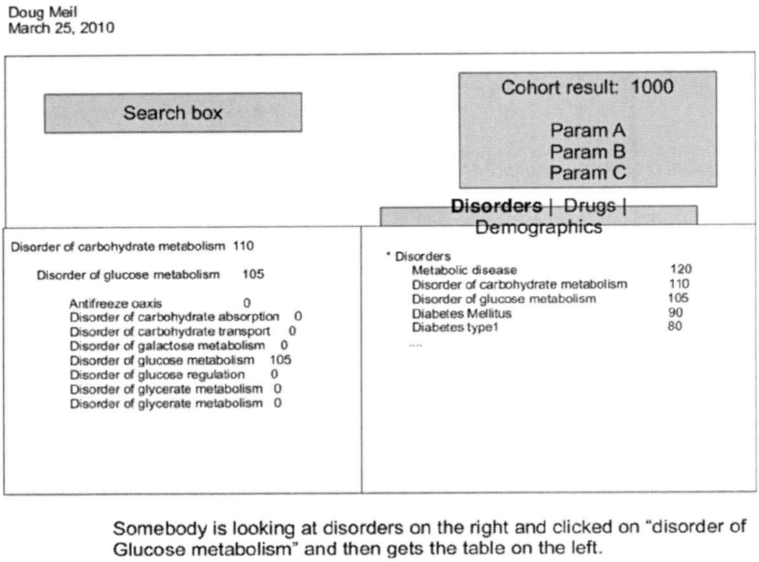

Figure A.1 My mockup of "Browse The Crowd" from March 2010. The comments at the bottom of the slide try to describe the intended user interaction. It wasn't fancy, but it got the job done. I don't remember where "Antifreeze oaxis" came from, though.

terminologies such as SNOMED, even though Explorys was only about six months old at this point. "FastSearch" was already in development with early working versions.

Explorys Memories – 1

Additional memories and reflections contributed from other Explorys team-members:

Dr Wleft

Late in the workday, we encountered a bug where a doctor named Dr Wright was erroneously showing up in Virtual Chart as "Dr. Wleft." We were aware of the obvious change from "right" to "left," but could not understand who would want to do that to a doctor's name.

It turns out a new developer was tasked to alter the alignment of some UI elements and did a full string replacement of the word "right" to the word "left" on the raw HTML.

In a normal codebase, that change might have worked well enough, but since this was a GWT application, HTML was frequently generated at runtime with the data already inside. So in addition to changing "text-align: right" to "text-align: left," "Dr. Wright" became "Dr. Wleft."

Subsidized Vending Machines

During our tenure at the Playhouse building, the company decided to add a subsidized snack vending machine where everything cost a quarter.

This was a decent little perk to have at the office. I would frequently get myself some Famous Amos cookies. Being a late worker than most, I would find myself at the office when the nightly cleaning crew would come in.

Over time, they eventually came to realize how cheap the snacks in the vending machine were.

There were multiple times members of the cleaning crew would go into the break room where the vending machine was and just repeatedly buy things and stuff the spoils in a garbage bag to take home.

Hearing the endless "coin drop" sound followed by the beeping and whirring of the vending machine was a regular part of the after hours ambience.

We made attempts to notify the front desk, who would then notify the cleaning company, but it kept on happening until IBM took over and the subsidized party was over.

The RDJ Readmission Usecase

Measuring readmissions is a very difficult task even in the simplest of use cases. A typical readmission involves being admitted to a facility, discharged with some diagnosis, and then admitted a second time within a set timeframe.

One use case Doug pointed out for us to watch out for is the "Robert Downey Jr" use case where you get admitted to rehab, sneak out the back door, get caught, and then admit back into rehab a second time.

This is not considered a valid readmission since the patient was never properly discharged.

I still laugh about that example anytime I deal with readmissions in my current work.

Team Breakpoint

At some point near the end of our time at GCIC, someone in management got the idea to have each team come up with a name for themselves.

The names were meant to not be tied directly to what products we were working on.

After a decent bit of deliberation on my team, we agreed to call ourselves "Team Breakpoint" (because breakpoints get it?).

Fast forward a few weeks, and the team names were locked in Team 1, Team 3, and Team Breakpoint.

Slack Snoopers

I didn't see this happen myself, but I have heard stories about how a high-level member of one of our co-acquirees in IBM Watson Health would snoop around our public "war room" chats in Slack.

They would then gather evidence to present to the higher-ups at IBM to present us in a bad light.

That kind of behavior set the stage for how some of the "divisions" of Watson Health treated each other.

Hopping Hadoop Distros

From the beginning, we were a CDH (Cloudera) shop through and through.

After IBM bought us out, we were tasked with converting to IBM's own Hadoop distro.

We then put in a good amount of effort to utilize said distro, only for IBM to initiate a partnership with Hortonworks, cancel their in-house distro, and have us pivot to HDP.

Moving to HDP was a rather painful process due to misalignment in software versions.

In particular, HBase would have been a very nasty version regression (internal serialization changes) unless we adopted the next HDP X.0 release, which was still in beta at the time.

After much hand-wringing, we went down that path.

It was a painful upgrade, and I've since learned to fear X.0 releases of critical infrastructure software, but we eventually got it stable.

Fast forward to Cloudera buying Hortonworks, and everything comes back to CDH except our cluster because it was left to rot at that point.

Pi Day

Data analysts are math nerds. They kinda have to be. One of our senior analysts was such a math nerd that he would set up a "Pi Day" on March 14th every year where people would bring in pies of their choice and we would have a banquet of sugar.

CDH4 (or 3?) Buttersticks

I don't remember which CDH upgrade (3 or 4), but one of the upgrades was a troublesome enough endeavor that a few engineers stayed all night at the office. I remember coming in on the weekend in an attempt to help out, only to find them raving about "Buttersticks."

While waiting for various upgrade tasks to finish, they apparently came up with a game where they threw leftover butter packets at a hole on a long table (that would normally be used for wire management) in effectively an extremely cheap iteration of shuffleboard.

Large platform upgrades do things to a person as I would learn in later platform upgrades.

Go to Sleep

I remember staying very late one workday (sometime after 12 am) working on some release related issue.

We were having trouble with our MySQL server (which we were grossly overloading with data at that point) and had a senior ops engineer (and resident DBA) on the phone. After getting to some form of resolution, I apologized from the depths of my heart for causing them to be up working so late.

Said engineer calmly replied with "It's OK, I wasn't going to go to sleep tonight anyways."

In a culmination of my frustrations leading up to that point, I simply responded "Fuck you. Go to sleep."

It's one of the very few times I dropped the F-bomb at a co-worker.

Aggressive Cornhole

Very early on in my career at Explorys, a few employees decided to set up a cornhole board down the main stretch of the office. Due to the shape of the office, there were desks (and people) directly to the left and right of the thoroughfare.

In a silly form of escalation, a few employees would continually push the cornhole board further and further back until they had to start doing softball-style pitches just to hit the board. This led to some near misses of equipment and people, and some employees started protesting the act.

One employee yelled "your cornhole is ravaging my productivity!"

A player responded with "your productivity is ravaging my cornhole!"

Said employee quickly realized the hilarity of their comment and stopped playing for the day.

Explorys Memories – 2

Additional memories and reflections contributed from other Explorys team-members:

New Grad at Explorys

Explorys/IBM (I joined post-acquisition) was my first job post-college, and I'll always be grateful to the Explorys team for giving me a shot. I was a biomedical engineering major trying to make a transition to software engineering, and most companies didn't want to even interview me because I was a "non-traditional" candidate. But I approached the Explorys booth at the Case Western Reserve University career fair and found an enthusiastic group that welcomed me despite the courses listed on my resume. Over the next few weeks, I passed two phone screens and an onsite technical + behavioral interview and found myself with an amazing offer. I still remember how excited I was; receiving that offer both completely altered and majorly accelerated the trajectory of my career.

Engines Team Memories

I was on the engines team at Explorys, which was a really tight-knit group, and a great environment for learning.

Frequently we paired with other teammates on projects, which helped me as the most junior member to learn good practices from the more experienced folks, particularly around system design, testing, and debugging. We also held team "learning sessions" each week, where someone from the team shared a presentation or demo of a new technology or topic they had learned recently or just found interesting.

And we did a lot of fun stuff as a team too! On an almost daily basis we played a round of MarioKart on Nintendo DS (which is wild to think about now, this was 2017!). I didn't even have one when I joined, but one of my team members lent me an extra he had so that I could play. That same team member later organized a Dominion tournament open to all of the Explorys engineers – I was terrible at Dominion at the time, but still had fun being a part of it. We also exchanged Christmas gifts every year, and we had plenty of happy hours and board game nights to remember. I think this experience kind of spoiled me because I haven't had such a close and fun team since!

Explorys Memories – 3

Additional memories and reflections contributed from other Explorys team-members:

I started at Explorys in the Summer of 2015 and I followed it until its decommissioning in 2022. The post Explorys emotions have been complex. Having seen other health data startups I'm amazed at how far ahead Explorys was. It's been almost a decade and I have yet to see anyone come close to the scale and capabilities. Other companies are still working on problems that Explorys solved before I started. I have feelings of pride and wonder at our accomplishments, but also grief as so much potential was lost.

Explorys Memories – 4

Additional memories and reflections contributed from other Explorys team-members:

It was a fantastic six years at Explorys, the last two at IBM, not so much. I learned a ton working with Doug and the team he built. Our team at Explorys was at the heart of two digital transformations. Explorys help enable transformation of the health care systems in the US from point of care to population management. And our technology and processes were best in class from source code management, and more to build and integration, continuous delivery, and all on top of the best platforms in the industry. Kudos to Doug for documenting, in this book, the Explorys story of our team leading and delivering the best healthcare digital transformation.

Explorys Memories – 5

Additional memories and reflections contributed from other Explorys team-members:

I first found out about Explorys at a job fair. This was in the Fall of 2009, at the heel of the housing crash so my optimism wasn't sky high. As a recent graduate, I knew that this was my best chance at finding employment.

The night before, I perused the list of companies that had registered for the event. IBM, Bloomberg, the big dogs. And then there was Explorys: a startup right here in Cleveland trying to tackle one of the most challenging problems in America: healthcare. I was hooked: the perfect marriage between data science, new tech, and medicine. I knew this was the company I needed to talk to.

At the day of job fair, I looked for their booth which to an untrained eye would have turned off most employment seeking recent graduates: instead of posters, they had three

8.5 × 11 inches pieces of papers with the words: BIG DATA, HADOOP, and Healthcare. And perhaps a slightly bigger piece of paper with the words Explorys. Sitting in their area was Doug Meil actively trying to recruit oblivious students walking by. Explorys wasn't flashy and this was intentional. Sure, it saves on costs, but I would like to think this was a deliberate decision to filter out prospective employees seduced by such trite measures.

What caught mine was that description from the job fair's pamphlet. No amount of 8.5 × 11 pieces of paper was going to deter me. After a short conversation with Doug Meil, I handed him my resume and walked on to the next company. That night, I followed up with an email explaining how excited I was to learn about the company and potential follow ups. Three weeks later, I met Charlie Lougheed at a Starbucks on West 6th in Cleveland: "I am sure you're probably interviewing other companies as we speak," he declared. I nodded. "Well, I just want you to know that of all the companies you are interviewing, Explorys is going to work you the most and pay you the least and I hope that's ok" he continued. I laughed. I was shocked, but yet intrigued at the same time. It takes a level of blatant honesty (perhaps naive) and courage to be able to blurt something like that. But it also spoke to the level of confidence they must have had with Explorys' premise. Whether Charlie was bluffing or not, it was hard not to be seduced by Explorys' potential.

I had met Steve, Doug, and Jason shortly later at various Starbucks locations around Cleveland.

And that was it: the entire interview process, done by the entire staff at the time. A few weeks later, I met Charlie a second time to sign the papers. He proudly brandishes a key: "This is a monumental moment for us" he announced as I looked curiously at the object he was gesturing. "We just signed the lease today, this is the key to our very first office!" This was news to me. They didn't have an office until just now. I felt sick. I had just turned down a lucrative offer from Bloomberg to join Explorys, and now I had questions. I felt like I had just gambled and I am not a gambling person. I had to take a leap of faith: *Alea iacta est*, I was about to cross the Rubicon.

My first day was Tuesday December 1st, 2009. The office was ground leveled with windows overlooking a common parking lot. Next to us was a UPS store, and a McDonalds several feet over. As I entered through the door, I couldn't help but feel like I was in an apartment. The large living room was the office space, the bedroom was the meeting room/ interview room. The room behind a giant glass door was the conference room. One unisex bathroom.

In that conference room sat Doug Meil, Charlie Lougheed, Steve McHale, and Jason Lotz discussing the future of the company. "So we need to talk about what kind of company we want to be" Steve said. "DAAS: Data As A Service" I remember Doug saying. As I looked in his direction holding a mug with the words: "A Cup of Shut the" two words, rhymes with cup and starts with an F. "DAAS? Mmh, I like that idea" Jason replied. "So guys, this should not come as a surprise, but we have enough funds to last until June of next year" Charlie revealed. I looked around the room and no one seemed very surprised. This was roughly seven months from now and that was 100% a surprise to me. "We have to deliver a product for our stakeholders that I've mocked in Dream Weaver" he proceeded to show us.

After that meeting, my very first task (which became an Explorys tradition with new hires) was to build my own desk. I am guessing they got this idea from Amazon. Charlie later joked that this should have been the job interview: if it takes you longer than four hours, you won't make it. Worst case scenario, we get new furniture.

For months Doug had architected the system's design, and data model. And finally, one glorious day, we had succeeded in running our very first Map Reduce job to generate indices over the entirety of our data set. At the time, we only had data from one healthcare network but it was still large enough that a traditional system's architecture couldn't handle it.

"Wow, it actually works?" Jason exclaimed in jubilation, almost incredulously. To be honest, we were all a little surprised. Like that chemistry experiment that finally gives you positive results after reading the lab details. From an idea to creation, a theory that became reality. This was the birth of something great.

Explorys grew exponentially for the first couple years. By January of 2010, we had nearly tripled in size, there were dozens of us. By the time we released our first product, right around June, we had reached 20.

One of the key moments in Explorys' track was convincing two rival healthcare networks to agree on using our platform. A common joke that was made on how the Ohio State–Michigan rivalry didn't hold a candle to the University Hospitals vs. Cleveland Clinic rivalry. I guess you would have to be a healthcare professional to get it. Or live in Cleveland for that matter. But somehow, we had done it.

When it comes to the healthcare industry, Cleveland is a bit of an outlier. For a city of its size, it's quite uncommon to have four major separate healthcare networks. But it worked to Explorys' advantage. It made our platform versatile enough and enriched our data enough to allow our data model and thus our products to mature before embarking into healthcare networks outside of Cleveland. By 2015, we had accounts from coast to coast, including Hawaii.

Albeit its tragic fate, Explorys did teach each of us things that cannot be taught elsewhere. It allowed me to pivot into a career in software engineering which I never thought was possible. I ended up working at Amazon Web Services at one point, being part of the Control Plane for the Elastic Block 9. core services. My story wasn't unique, as many of us ended up finding successful paths in tech as more than few went to companies like Google, Facebook, Amazon, and Elastic. The Explorys engineering experience carried a lot of credibility.

It is a bit curious how a small company off of Cleveland, Ohio ended up doing so well and I often respond with: "we had the right people: kind, smart, voracious learners, curious individuals, willing to teach and mentor others." We had hired engineers that way. Talent, skills, and experience weren't enough: if that person was, say, an egomaniac, it wouldn't fit our culture and they wouldn't be hired.

The culture was such that it taught us to believe in ourselves and persevere. It empowered each one of us to come up with engineering solutions that could dramatically affect the business. We were disciplined but also dynamic enough that we could pivot if need be. I have worked for two more startups after that, none had done quite as well as Explorys. I will forever be grateful.

Explorys Memories – 6

Additional memories and reflections contributed from other Explorys team-members:

There are two stories that stick out in my memories for how much being acquired by a large company affected the spirit of what we did at Explorys.

Early on during my time at Explorys, we had a tranche milestone that we needed to meet in order to unlock funding. It was early December and we had just two possible clients that would help us meet the milestone. One client was in Hawaii and was dragging their feet committing to a contract. Our other client was within driving distance of our offices and was very interested, but given their lengthy contracting process, we were unlikely to close the deal and get our technical work done if we waited until the contract was signed to start the tech work. My boss and myself decided to do something to help ensure we could meet our milestone even if the contract was signed very late in December. We decided to work on getting our servers installed ahead of the contract being finalized. We knew this was a bit risky, since our work may rankle the leadership of the hospital. We decided to keep things very high touch and personal with our IT contacts. So I drove our server, rather than ship it, to the client's data center. Initially, the IT staff was a bit skeptical, but we assured them that we just wanted to avoid holiday shipping delays. A day later, I called our contact and asked if he would rack the server, but not turn it on, again letting him know it was out of concern for him and having to work late near or over the holidays. Finally, I called again and asked if he would turn the server on and connect it to their network so we could ensure the server works, again so we don't have to bother him over the holidays. He obliged again. Bingo, we were setup and ready to go. The contract was signed with just a few days left to meet our milestone, had we waited, we would never have been able to meet the milestone. However, because of our scrappy moves to get the server installed, we were able to meet our milestones. As a celebration, my boss brought in Pappy Van Winkle, before it was nigh unobtainable, and I proceeded to have a few Pappy Noggs on the last day before holiday vacations. It felt amazing, I felt like I had made a difference.

Now, let's move several years forward. We were in the middle of the "Blue Washing" IBM onboarding process. One of the most painful parts was cataloging our offerings and making part numbers out of them. This was done so the IBM global workforce could, in theory, sell our products and services to their clients. In practice, this made no sense, since our solution was not self-service and integrating with a health system required a deep knowledge of their IT systems to determine the effort required.

IBM was insistent, so we went along. Step one was to take our current client work and break it apart into distinct parts numbers. The idea being that common tasks we had done at each company would have a common part number. This, of course, doesn't really make sense when you are talking about a startup working in a healthcare space where each client has different needs. So in essence, we built a one of one solution for each client using a standard tech platform to deliver it. One way of thinking of it is how AWS has a common tech platform, but each website or service built using it is unique. So were in a meeting and one of our VPs is going through and explaining the work done for a client, and the IBM people were getting frustrated that each client is different enough that we need a new part number. Also, our VP was frustrated having to defend why we did things the way we did, because the answer was "we were a startup, we did what we had to in order to please clients and survive." So one client's work came up and our VP just said this was a one off research project and we should just look at it as hours billed, plus a core tech fee. An IBM staffer asked how customers ordered from Explorys, and our VP's answer was they came to us with a budget and an ask, so we worked with them to get what they wanted done. The IBM staffer said "you can't do that." Our VP said "So if a client comes to me with 3 million dollars and an idea, if I don't have a part number, we can't help them?" The IBM staffer said "correct, you can't sell something that doesn't have a part number." Right then and there, I knew Explorys was dead. That scrappy startup where I was told "understand our client's process, but don't be beholden to it," was no more. I decided to leave shortly after.

Explorys Memories – 7

Additional memories and reflections contributed from other Explorys team-members:

The Screwdriver

Explorys bought our desks from IKEA. Part of your first day on the job was assembling the desk; nothing too tricky, but you needed a screwdriver (in addition to the IKEA Allen wrench) to put it together. This *became* tricky for one of the newest team members, an insanely talented programmer, right out of college. He got all of the parts out and was ready to start assembling the desk, but couldn't find a screwdriver. He came to me to ask if I knew anyone who had one. I gave him a name. He went and talked to that person, who said no, but gave him another name. This went on down a list of 20 people; no one had a screwdriver. He came back to me with the report and I was utterly confused. We went to the DevOps room together and asked for a screwdriver – they begrudgingly let him borrow their last one – they had all been lost over time. Luckily Explorys kept better care of its data than its screwdrivers.

For the months/years that followed that new employee was convinced that the screwdriver was an onboarding tactic to get them to meet a bunch of the existing employees. Unfortunately it wasn't that complex, it was simply a screwdriver and a desk.

Billing History

I joined Explorys working part time as a grad student. This was my first job in a startup environment and I had imposter syndrome from the first day. Explorys was stacked with technical talent and I was just happy to be there.

One of my first assignments was implementing a parser and grouper for billing data. For those not familiar, medical billing data is among the most complex, one of the books on the topic says it is harder than rocket science. Of course I didn't know this at the time and naively opened up the 512 page X12 manual on the topic and read it cover to cover. When I asked others some clarifying questions about the details/who I could follow up with the answer became terrifyingly apparent: I *was* the Explorys expert on billing data at the time. There was a problem with that: I barely knew what I was doing. Of course, like any startup story I didn't have a ton of time to figure things out – we had already committed delivery to a client in a few short months.

I quickly got to work writing the parser and testing it against data. I hit problem after problem trying to get it off the ground – it is worth noting here – I am not the best programmer in the world, but I make up for it in sheer grit and time. Oh so much time. What followed was a grueling couple months of work where I was pulling 18+ hour days getting the integration right. How do I know I was working 18+ hours? Because at the same time we had just implemented time tracking software. The last few weeks were a blur running up to the deadline, but I managed to get it out the door and my coworker nailed the accompanying UI (and helped me on the backend too – thanks man).

At the end of all of this I was a mess. I hadn't slept, the code worked just enough and we delivered on time or late-ish – honestly I don't remember at this point. What I do remember is our VP of engineering calling me into his office along with my boss a couple weeks after delivery. My heart was RACING. I legitimately thought I was going to be fired for ineffectiveness (see imposter syndrome above). Instead though, the VP listed out a bunch of numbers, all below 24. He asked me what I thought they were – I was so confused and tired I had no idea. They apparently were the daily reports of how many hours I was pulling. He thanked me for the hard work and results. I shook their hands and made my way to the hallway where the exhaustion, emotion of the meeting, and everything came out in tears. This would be the first, but not the last time I cried while at Explorys.

Explorys Memories – 8

Additional memories and reflections contributed from other Explorys team-members:

I began my career, straight out of school, working at Explorys as a junior developer at the very beginning of 2012. I stayed with Explorys and then IBM Watson health for about seven years, and am grateful to have had the opportunity to grow in my career and learn from the amazing group of talent that made up Explorys. I have continued a career in the same field – processing large healthcare datasets – for a number of companies, including start-ups and huge corporations. However, over the past several years, I have found myself reminiscing with old acquaintances on how that first job at Explorys was the best, most enjoyable job I ever had.

Until the time of my departure from IBM Watson Health, Explorys/IBM Watson Health was all I ever knew in industry – I really didn't have any other experience to compare it against. It was really only after I had other experiences to compare it to that I realized just how far ahead of its time Explorys was and how top-notch the talent was. Nothing is ever perfect – especially when you are in the midst of it. There were always things we wanted to be faster, more reliable, more feature rich – and we were continually chasing after that. So, in the moment, things always felt like they could be better. It was only when I saw the problems to be solved at subsequent employers that I realized just how far ahead of the curve Explorys was. As subsequent post-Explorys teams I was on struggled to semi-automate, test, speed up, and build operations around data processes, I was struck with the realization that we were processing datasets several orders of magnitude larger, reliably, with appropriate testing, and significantly faster at Explorys – almost as an afterthought – a decade earlier!

In addition to this, we were able to evolve our data platform significantly over time to help enable internal data scientists/engineers to be much more self-serve with data processing capabilities. This type of transformation can be extraordinarily difficult to complete in organizations big and small even with the multitude of web services available today, and we were doing this all before the time of all of the off-the-shelf solutions available from AWS, GCP, and the like (or at least before they had HIPAA compliant solutions).

It was really a great place to grow up as a young professional. We had the talent to both develop fantastic technical solutions, but also a team which worked well enough together to really be able to make big changes across the platform successfully. It is a shame to think what might have been achievable, especially after having seen how other firms struggle to do even small portions of what Explorys did successfully and the eventual fate of Explorys. It was a sad, but somewhat fitting end to my time at IBM Watson Health (given the eventual fate of IBM Watson Health) that the one project keeping me at IBM Watson Health and excited (which included near-real time data processing and more) was cancelled shortly after my departure. A lot of time, effort, and potential wasted – a seemingly suitable metaphor for the IBM Watson Health venture at large.

A Few More Pictures

I just had to include a few more pictures of the Old Cleveland Playhouse. It's still hard to believe we actually worked in this place. Jen Hearn was a former Explorys employee who also had a sharp eye with a camera for unconventional and behind-the-scenes perspectives.

Figure A.2 One of the back stairwells in the Old Cleveland Playhouse (2013). This was supposed to be one of the "emergency escape routes" but it wasn't entirely clear where this went. Permission from Jen Hearn.

Figure A.3 A hallway in the Old Cleveland Playhouse (2013) that we all walked past to get to the Explorys office. Permission from Jen Hearn.

Figure A.4 One of the original theaters in the Old Cleveland Playhouse (2013). There were four theaters, I think, in the complex plus a black box theater. Permission from Jen Hearn.

Figure A.5 The library of the Old Cleveland Playhouse (2013). We used to have large-group meetings in here, and one time a pane of glass from the upper-level bookcase dislodged during one of those meetings and missed someone by inches. Good times! Permission from Jen Hearn.

Figure A.6 The third floor of the Old Cleveland Playhouse (2013). This was the floor directly above Explorys and had trash cans for rain collection and some birds as tenants. Permission from Jen Hearn.

Comments on Medical Terminologies

SNOMED

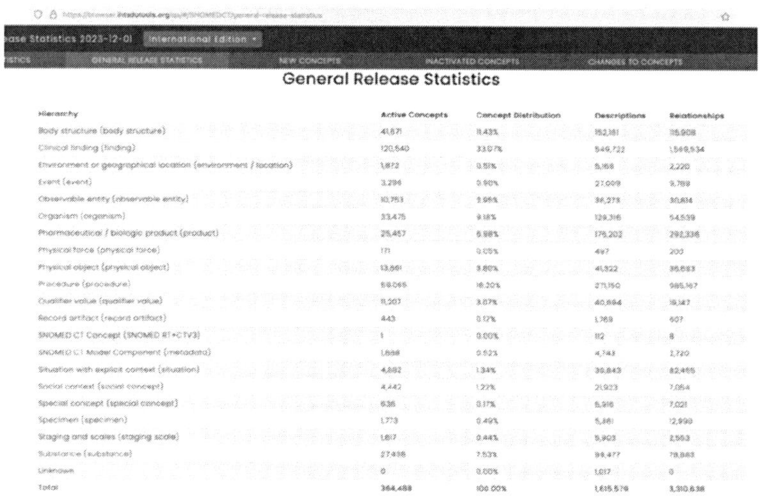

General Release Statistics

Hierarchy	Active Concepts	Concept Distribution	Descriptions	Relationships
Body structure (body structure)	41,871	11.43%	152,181	35,908
Clinical finding (finding)	120,540	33.07%	546,722	1,569,534
Environment or geographical location (environment / location)	1,872	0.51%	5,168	2,220
Event (event)	3,294	0.90%	27,009	9,789
Observable entity (observable entity)	10,753	2.95%	36,275	30,614
Organism (organism)	33,475	9.18%	129,316	54,539
Pharmaceutical / biologic product (product)	25,457	6.98%	176,202	292,336
Physical force (physical force)	171	0.05%	497	200
Physical object (physical object)	13,861	3.80%	41,322	36,683
Procedure (procedure)	59,065	16.20%	271,150	985,167
Qualifier value (qualifier value)	11,207	3.07%	40,894	19,147
Record artifact (record artifact)	443	0.12%	1,769	607
SNOMED CT Concept (SNOMED RT+CTV3)	1	0.00%	112	8
SNOMED CT Model Component (metadata)	1,888	0.52%	4,743	2,720
Situation with explicit context (situation)	4,882	1.34%	30,843	82,465
Social context (social concept)	4,442	1.22%	21,923	7,054
Special concept (special concept)	636	0.17%	5,916	7,021
Specimen (specimen)	1,773	0.49%	5,361	12,990
Staging and scales (staging scale)	1,617	0.44%	5,903	2,563
Substance (substance)	27,438	7.53%	99,477	78,863
Unknown	0	0.00%	1,017	0
Total	364,488	100.00%	1,615,576	3,310,838

Figure A.7 SNOMED CT concept statistics (February 2024) – https://browser.ihtsdotools.org/qa/#/SNOMEDCT/general-release-statistics

SNOMED is big. Really big. The Clinical Finding sub-graph is 120.5k concepts, and the Procedure sub-graph is about 60k concepts. The Substance (27.4k) and Product (25.5k) sub-graphs were also used by Explorys as well for drug classifications. Note that the descriptions, which would include aliases and synonyms, are even more numerous than their respective concepts.

Back when we were designing Population Explorer at Explorys in early 2010, I had a funny exchange with Cleveland Clinic research coordinators about this kind of layout, as the current SNOMED browser looks like the old Population Explorer concept browser. The research coordinator was confused with the concept browser and asked "how do you know the children have Diabetes?" and "how do you know the parents have an endocrine disorder?" I was with another senior software engineer, and we glanced back and forth trying to figure out where the confusion was. Although SNOMED had been around for years, it was still relatively niche at that point and the research coordinators weren't familiar with using it.

Then it hit us: the research coordinators thought they were selecting attributes of a *single patient* (e.g., "patients with diabetes who also have a child with diabetes"). We changed the labels in the concept browser from "parents" and "children" to "more general" and "more specific" and that seemed to resolve the confusion, and that's the way the labels stayed for the life of the product.The irony is that SNOMED has "parents" and "children" labels like we had in our very first implementation.

Population Explorer also misused epidemiological words in various places. A cohort, strictly speaking, is a group of people in a study who are monitored over time, like the famous

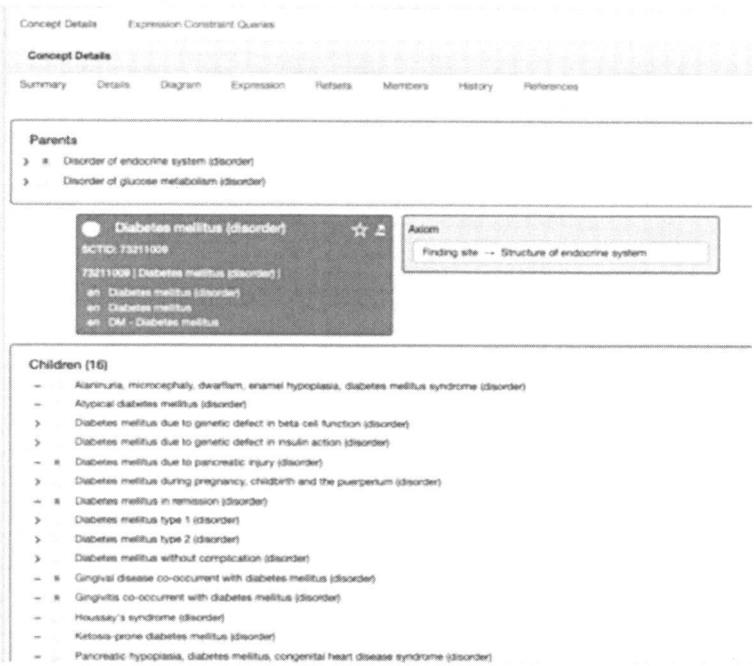

Figure A.8 Diabetes mellitus in SNOMED. (https://browser.ihtsdotools.org)

Framingham Study. Cohorts are forward-looking, so to speak. A case-control study is backward-looking. Population Explorer used “cohort” to mean any query in the tool. Population Explorer also used “baseline” in a non-standard way in PowerSearch to mean anything that wasn’t temporally specified. Apologies to any epidemiologists that we offended. We were learning on the fly.

RxNorm

Explorys initially went live with a proprietary drug database for drug metadata in 2010, but we switched it out to RxNorm in the Spring of 2011 due to an inability to come to contract terms. The vendor went from wanting not so much money to https://www.nlm.nih.gov/research/umls/sourcereleasedocs/current/RXNORM/stats.html

RXNORM (RXNORM) - Statistics

Synopsis Metadata Statistics Source Representation Metathesaurus Representation

Semantic Type Distribution

Semantic Type ID	Semantic Type Name	Count	Percentage Distribution
T200	Clinical Drug	185369	75.4
T121	Pharmacologic Substance	26205	10.7
T109	Organic Chemical	23122	9.4

Term Type Counts

Term Type	Expanded Form	Count
SY	Designated synonym	63502
SCD	Semantic Clinical Drug	38428
PSN	Prescribable Names	35792
SCDC	Semantic Drug Component	27500
TMSY	Tall Man synonym	26621
SBD	Semantic branded drug	22696
SBDG	Semantic branded drug group	19522
SBDC	Semantic Branded Drug Component	18620
SCDG	Semantic clinical drug group	16051
SCDF	Semantic clinical drug and form	14771
IN	Name for an ingredient	14171
SBDF	Semantic branded drug and form	14034
BN	Fully-specified drug brand name that can not be prescribed	11431
SBDFP	Semantic branded drug and form with precise ingredient as basis of strength	4887

Figure A.9 RxNorm statistics (February 2024). https://www.nlm.nih.gov/research/umls/sourcereleasedocs/current/RXNORM/stats.html

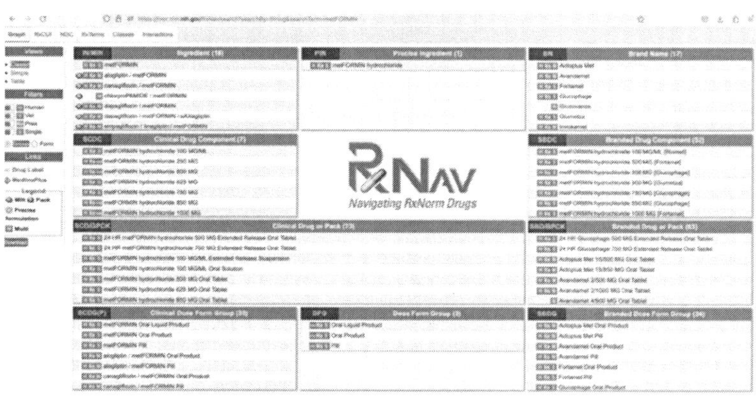

Figure A.10 Metformin example in RxNav.

wanting a lot of money. If anything, this vendor did us a favor by doing this in 2011 because Explorys only had one product at the time.

Although not as big as SNOMED, there is still a lot to drug metadata: 14k ingredients, 35k prescribable names, and 63.5k synonyms. And this doesn't even include NDCs (National Drug Codes).

LOINC

LOINC had been around for over 15 years by the time Explorys started working with it in 2009 and had about 42k laboratory concepts and almost 15k non-lab concepts at that time. But it did not then have widespread adoption, and Explorys had to do a lot of data standardization. A red blood cell count was encoded as "RBC" in one hospital but as "EBC" in another, since erythrocyte also meant red blood cells. White blood cells and leukocytes are another such instance. Explorys had to map a great many source values to their LOINC equivalents.

At the time of writing as of end 2023, LOINC has almost 62k laboratory concepts and 40k non-lab concepts.

As with SNOMED and RxNorm, there are concepts and then there are the details behind the concepts, and LOINC is no exception, including attributes like component/analyte (the thing being analyzed), property, time unit, system (i.e., of the body), scale, and method.

Figure A.11 LOINC release history and number of terms (February 2024). https://loinc.org/history/

Figure A.12 LOINC example (LOINC.org).

Index